BUILD YOUR OWN BRAND

STRATEGIES, PROMPTS AND EXERCISES FOR MARKETING YOURSELF

ROBIN LANDA

Cincinnati, Ohio
www.howdesign.com

Build Your Own Brand. Copyright © 2013 by Robin Landa. Manufactured in China. All rights reserved. No other part of this book may be reproduced in any form or by any electronic or mechanical means including information storage and retrieval systems without permission in writing from the publisher, except by a reviewer, who may quote brief passages in a review. Published by HOW Books, an imprint of F+W Media, Inc., 10151 Carver Road, Suite 200, Blue Ash, Ohio 45242. (800) 289-0963. First edition.

For more excellent books and resources for designers, visit www.howdesign.com.

17 16 15 14 13   5 4 3 2 1

ISBN-13: 978-1-4403-2455-0

Distributed in Canada by Fraser Direct
100 Armstrong Avenue
Georgetown, Ontario, Canada L7G 5S4
Tel: (905) 877-4411

Distributed in the U.K. and Europe by F&W Media International, LTD
Brunel House, Forde Close, Newton Abbot, TQ12 4PU, UK
Tel: (+44) 1626 323200, Fax: (+44) 1626 323319
Email: enquiries@fwmedia.com

Distributed in Australia by Capricorn Link
P.O. Box 704, Windsor, NSW 2756 Australia
Tel: (02) 4560-1600

EDITOR	Scott Francis
DESIGNER	Ronson Slagle
PRODUCTION COORDINATOR	Greg Nock
ILLUSTRATOR	Allison Kerek

Dedication
TO YOUR BRILLIANT CAREER

"**KNOWLEDGE** IS IN THE END BASED ON ACKNOWLEDGMENT."

LUDWIG WITTGENSTEIN

Acknowledgments

As it happens, showing my gratitude makes me feel really good, therefore the generous people who have already contributed to this book are still helping me. For all their help, I extend a huge thank you in reverse alphabetical order because I felt badly about the people with *W* names who usually are listed almost last. (My guess is everyone would probably prefer a modest thank-you gift, such as a bottle of Dom Pérignon, rather than this acknowledgment but here remains my appreciation.)

Melanie Wiesenthal
Rob Wallace
Laurence Vincent
Dr. Jeffrey Toney
Kelly Thorn
John Sposato
Seunghyun Shon
Ronson Slagle
Mike Sickinger
Joe Schwartz
Karen Sonet Rosenthal
Alberto Romanos
Deborah Ceballos Rivera
Paul Renner
Dr. Kristie Reilly
Manik Rathee
Jaime Lynn Pescia

Megan Lane Patrick
Amy Owen
Nancy Novick
Dr. Richard L. Nochimson
Dr. Julia Nevárez
Debbie Millman
Kevin McCloskey
Holly Logue
Steve Liska
Dany Lennon
Margrethe Lauber
Lorin Latarro
Alessandra Lariu
Rudyard Kipling
Stephen King
Sean King
Allison Kerek

Pete Jones
Simon Helberg
Andrea Cohen Harris
Stephen Thomas Hall
Hayley Gruenspan
Dr. Harry Gruenspan
Dr. Zandra Gratz
Rose Gonnella
Jim Godfrey
Dr. Susan Gannon
Scott Francis
Lindy Foreman
Don Fishbein
Dr. Dawood Farahi
Grace Duong
Alice Drueding
Dr. Steven Doloff

Drew Davies
Jon Contino
Brian Collins
Lee Clow
Kristen Campolattaro
Steven Brower
Dr. Linda Breskin
Dr. Suzanne Bousquet
Gui Borchert
Matteo Bologna
Dr. Jill Bellinson
Kenny Barela
Dean James Ballas
Rich Arnold
Dr. George Z. Arasimowicz
Denise Anderson
Sean Adams

Table of Contents

Chapter One: Your Unique Sense and Sensibility 10

Branding 11
Your Vision 17
Archetypes 18
Complements 19
Associations 19
Ethical Virtues 20
Demonstration 21
The Quest or "What's My Style?" 22
Evaluating Your Premise 24
Personal Projects 24
Prompts 27

Chapter Two: Verbal Identity 56

What's In a Name? 56
Liberating Your Inner Writer 58
Telling Your Story 60
Elevator Speech 64
Tools to Aid Crafting Your Verbal Brand 66
Résumé and Cover Letter 69
Conventional Résumé Contents 70
Twitter 73
Prompts 78

Chapter Three: Visual Identity 104

Visualizing Your Brand Story 104
Logo: Telling Your Visual Story 110
Type and Image Relationship in a Logo 111
Color 114
Résumé, Letterhead and Business Card 118
Website 125
Prompts 128

Chapter Four: Case Studies 156

Debbie Millman 157	Kelly Thorn 186
Paul Renner 162	Kenny Barela 190
Rich Arnold 166	Jim Godfrey 194
Seunghyun Shon 170	Jon Contino 198
Manik Rathee 174	Allison Kerek 204
Grace Duong 180	Gui Borchert 208
Michael Sickinger 184	

Chapter Five: Resources 214

Color 215	Type Glossary 224
Glossary of Symbols 218	Glossary of Terms 228
Visualization Techniques 219	

Permissions 230
About the Author 231
Index 232

> "TO BE YOURSELF IN A WORLD THAT IS CONSTANTLY TRYING TO MAKE YOU SOMETHING ELSE IS THE GREATEST ACCOMPLISHMENT."
> RALPH WALDO EMERSON

CHAPTER ONE

YOUR UNIQUE SENSE AND SENSIBILITY

> "NEVER FORGET THAT BUILDING YOUR OWN BRAND IS ABOUT DETERMINING THE THINGS THAT MAKE YOU DIFFERENT FROM EVERY OTHER DESIGNER, AND SHINING A WHITE-HOT SPOTLIGHT ON THEM."
> DREW DAVIES, OWNER, OXIDE DESIGN CO.

BRANDING

What if people could evaluate your talent and skill based only on shapes and colors? What if people could understand your essence through one visual symbol? Or a short social media profile?

That is the task—to build a personal (subjective) visual identity from symbolic graphic elements and parts. Define your essence through design and words. Define your essence in a few shapes. The resulting shapes may look deceptively simple because they are a result of a complex distillation process, a concentrated condensation of who you are into a design. To develop and produce a visual and verbal response to a personal identity communication problem, you must discern meaning from information, go through creative and conceptual processes drawing upon information, research and iterations of creations boiled down into a solution, which has been shaped by layers of meaning. Every word and every graphic element tells.

You may not feel like a brand. You're an individual, not a cookie or a car. You may not even be a big fan of using branding terms for individuals—not even for famous individuals such as Jennifer Lopez or John Grisham.

To secure a creative career, however, you have to be a "recognizable type of something," which is how one dictionary defines brand. To break through, you need to make an indelible impression on your audience. And that's what this book will help you do.

Building your own brand entails using your design expertise to create an original visual and verbal identity for yourself. You are not a corporation so your identity should not look like a corporate identity. Nor are you exactly like every other designer, so your bio shouldn't read like anyone else's. Your typography, composition and copy should reflect your design sense and sensibility. There are many admirable portfolios out there. An engaging personal brand identity can ensure notice of yours.

TRANSMEDIA STORYTELLING

Creating a transmedia personal branding program entails weaving some common threads through all visual and verbal components across media, with the understanding that each medium can offer unique brand experiences for the audience. This means you have to formulate and create a strategic and unified program. Rather than approaching individual formats (such as your visual identity or website design) as isolated design solutions, it is a strategic imperative to see every expression and platform—from the visual identity to the self-promotions—as a contributor to the entire branding. This cohesive approach is critical to creating an experience based on your unique visual and verbal presence.

Why do you need to tell a story? Context. Human interest. *A brand story tells the world precisely who you are and what you have to offer.*

Whether in the form of song lyrics (regardless of genre—rock, rap, opera, pop, R&B, country); fiction or films, documentaries or video games, people love stories and find meaning in stories.

There's a reason you see human interest stories on the news. In his book, *The Storytelling Animal: How Stories Make Us Human*, Jonathan Gottschall writes, "Human minds yield helplessly to the suction of story."

People more easily remember a story well told as opposed to remembering a list or facts. Gottschall writes, "We all have a life story that defines us—a narrative that describes who we are and how we got this way. But our comically unreliable self-narration is underpinned by boldly fictionalized memories. We are our stories, and those stories are more truthy than true." *(http://jonathangottschall.com/big-ideas/)*

To tell a story, you don't have to be a writer. A single image can tell a story. Image plus words can tell a story, as they do in advertising or single-panel cartoons (just think of *The New Yorker* cartoons) or on book covers or posters. Certainly, we can also use motion graphics or an illustration to tell a story.

The cumulative effect of a visual and verbal identity tells a story about your personality, sense, sensibility, skills—it defines you and how you got that way. Can you literally tell a story? Sure. Can you tell a story cobbled together with words and images? Of course. Forming a story as the underpinning of what you do will help congeal your identity, help people seize on your identity. You are the lead character in this story.

YOUR STRATEGY

Strategy is the core tactical underpinning of branding, uniting all your planning for every visual and verbal expression. The brand strategy defines your personality and promise. Who are you? What value do you promise to deliver?

Strategy also differentiates you from the competition by defining your "position" against the competition. You can formulate a construct—a core strategic concept that positions you (in an employer's or client's mind) against the competition—based on any insight into your own qualities or expertise, or on a personal attribute, such as originality, heritage, wit, or wisdom.

Several factors must be considered when formulating your strategy:

Differentiation: You create a unique visual and verbal presence.

Authenticity/Ownership: You "own" an identifiable attribute, quality, personality, or posture.

Consistency: Your construct is used across media, creating a coherent personal brand voice and tone in all verbal and visual communication. (Don't think of it as "matched luggage" but there should be coherence.)

Relevance: The branding is based on an insight into you *and* your target audience.

ADVICE FROM ALBERTO ROMANOS
HTTP://ALBERTOROMANOS.COM

Designing your personal brand is arguably the toughest task for a designer, as you are your own client. You might think you know yourself very well, but you will be surprised.

It´s not who you think you are, but what others will think you are. The closer these two things are, the better you have managed to do it.

ASK YOURSELF:

What are your values? What is your approach? Pick what is differentiating and likeable out of your answers and run with them.

Ask yourself where your brand is going to live; where are the touch points? You might need business cards, but you will also have to consider social media and portfolio websites, or even the emails you send, where there's little room for customization.

VISUALLY SPEAKING:

Do you really need a logo? Do you wear the same shirt every day?

If you go for a logo, do you need to explain it? Yes? Start again.

As well as the visual side of it, think about the tone of voice. Think about the media that fits your personality best.

—**ALBERTO ROMANOS**

Codify who you are, your promise, and your position into a core concept that becomes your strategy. To determine your strategy, it helps to answer some key questions in the form of a design brief:

Question 1: What is your goal? Specifically articulate your aim.

Question 2: Who is the core audience? Identify the people who comprise your core audience in order to form relevant design concepts.

Question 3: What would you like the core audience to think about you? Determine one clear thought you want the audience to have when they experience your brand identity.

Question 4: What is the key emotion that will build a relationship with the core audience? Identify one emotion that people ought to feel most about you from the brand experiences you construct.

Question 5: What specific information, concepts, visuals and design will assist in this? Ensure people form an accurate and positive opinion of you based on your visual and verbal identity.

Question 6: What is at the core of your brand personality? Form one well-defined authentic essence.

Question 7: What media will best facilitate your goal? Where do the people you want to reach spend the most time?

Question 8: What is your budget? Budget affects media selection and will affect many of your other decisions, including the cost of building a website, paper selection or substrates for print, as well as the number of colors for print.

Question 9: What is the single most important take away? Establish the single most important message to convey in the form of a single thought.

Question 10: What do you want the audience to do? Define the call to action. (Does your self-promotional piece drive people to visit your website, or to call you, or to email you?)

> **"A BRAND IDENTITY IS A LOT MORE COMPLEX THAN WHAT YOU FEEL OR HAVE DONE, IT IS IN FACT HOW YOU THINK!"**
> DANY LENNON, FOUNDER/PRESIDENT, THE CREATIVE REGISTER

GOALS OF A PERSONAL BRAND IDENTITY

Strategically, a visual identity should be:

- **Identifiable:** The design is distinguishable (it's yours and not John's or Maria's or wouldn't easily fit a thousand other designers).
- **Memorable:** The verbal components and the visual (type, imagery and color palette) are coherent and easily remembered.
- **Distinctive:** The name, shapes, forms and colors are uniquely characteristic to you and differentiate you from the competition.
- **Flexible:** The design and copy are tailored for specific media and flexible enough to be tailored for each medium.

ABOUT YOU

If you have a point of departure to determine your visual and verbal identity, that's good—start there. If you don't, this chapter offers many ways to develop one.

Nearly any "About Me" section of a website is dull (as well as too long) when it could be fascinating or clever—an authentic statement about the individual. Any personal brand identity is an "About Me" enterprise. So let's tackle this aspect first. Let's dissect you:

- **Your training:** your sense, what you know, your collective educational experiences, how you think, how you see, how you visualize what you see
- **Your personality:** your epitomizing traits
- **Your promise:** what you will deliver as a result of your expertise: your insights, designs, writing, art and code, creations
- **Your artistic vision:** your sensibility, what you bring to the party, your unique point of view, how you think, design, and how you perceive things

Bring these four components together to develop your "About Me" story. The final form of the narrative may be a synthesis of these components or a combination of them. It's also possible that only one component will communicate well enough to represent you. Twist or turn them. Edit. Delete. Combine.

PAINTING A DESIGNER'S SELF-PORTRAIT

"Who am I as a designer?" and "How can I communicate who I am?" are not easy questions for most of us to answer. Perhaps related questions can help you articulate answers to these questions:

- What are two or three distinctive traits, or ways of thinking or creating that make me the designer I am?
- How do I want to present myself professionally?
- How do I want people to perceive me?
- How can I visually express those qualities that make me distinctive?
- Can I incorporate different sides of myself? Should I?

- As a creative thinker, how am I changing from year to year?
- What kind of designer do I want to become?
- Do I need to reimagine, recast, or reinvent myself? How?

FUNCTIONAL AND EMOTIONAL BENEFITS

If many designers or writers or illustrators have excellent portfolio content, why would a potential employer choose one over another? Whim? Looking for a specific aesthetic or skill set?

In the marketplace, you are the sum total of your functional and emotional assets. You offer functional benefits to an employer—meaning practical skills or capabilities or sense—which may or may not be unique to you. For example, you may be able to design and write code; or design and hand letter; or you may be able to write copy in English as well as in Chinese.

You also have intangible assets—emotional assets—communicated through the design and verbal components of your identity. For example, the emotional tone of your design and copy may be humorous or mischievous.

ALTERING YOUR SELF-PORTRAIT

Alex Osborn, who first developed the idea of brainstorming, created the following checklist to transform an existent idea or object. To see yourself anew, you can try applying these actions to any benefit or element of your identity.

- **Adapt:** Adjust or rethink an element to meet a requirement.
- **Modify:** Alter an element.
- **Magnify:** Enlarge, expand, or overstate an element.
- **Minimize:** Reduce, understate or make an element smaller.
- **Substitute:** Replace a component.
- **Rearrange:** Change the order of components.
- **Reverse:** Change an element to its opposite.

PERSONAL BRANDING
STEVE LISKA, OWNER, LISKA + ASSOCIATES

Branding is about experience. What do people experience when they see, meet or work with you? Write it down.

- What are the top five things that define you? These are your brand attributes. Are they unique? Rate them.
- Thinking about the companies you want to work with. How does your personal brand sync with theirs?
- Who is your competition? How are you similar/different?
- Articulate your value to a client. Be objective.
- You already are your personal brand. What needs to change?

> "**When** interviewing, of course I want to know that you do great work, but I also want to know that you are a great person, a person that I can spend every day with. And a person that I can trust to do the right thing."
>
> Jaime Lynn Pescia, Art Director, Designer, Educator

Your Vision

What is your vision and how can you communicate it to others?

- Do you see beauty in the ordinary?
- Are you good at finding insights?
- Does your working method define your vision?
- Is your vision affected by your culture? By your training? By a limited palette of form? By a commitment to green design and sustainability?
- Is your vision as simple as being a type maven or as complex as holding to a philosophy of aesthetics?
- Do you search for truth? Do you have a specific aesthetic?
- Are you attracted to certain forms, shapes, color palettes, or points of view in the arts?

> "**Pick a CD cover that is your personification. Figure out why.**"
>
> Steve Liska, Owner, Liska + Associates

Most every design school graduate who was paying attention graduates with a set of skills. These skills range from type skills to utilizing a grid to building wireframes. Determining one's own aesthetic is another matter and perhaps one that can aid casting a personal brand.

ARCHETYPES

Brands attract specific audiences for a variety of reasons: status, quality and what each brand represents. Do you think Apple projects the image of the archetypal outlaw? Does the Nike brand project the archetype of a hero? Many people resonate with certain archetypes, predicting their own affinities and life themes. Perhaps one of the exemplary archetypes shown here will allow you to better understand your own personality and how to express it to others.

Creator: Characterized by being innovative, imaginative and artistic; a nonconformist who appreciates aesthetics

Explorer: Characterized by adventurousness, by being inquisitive and free-willed

Hero: Characterized by a symbolic expression of courage; triumph over adversity—one against the universe, a defining struggle of existence

Innocent: Characterized by being pure, perhaps naïve; one who longs for simplicity

Jester: Characterized by playfulness or being mischievous, loving fun and frivolity; sometimes ironic

Lover: Characterized by sensuality, intense interest in romance; very passionate

Outlaw: Characterized by being rebellious, breaking rules; self-defined, wild or an iconoclast

Magician: Characterized by an interest in transformations and metamorphoses, alchemy or represented by a conjurer or scientist (chemist or physicist)

Sage: Characterized by valuing truth and seeking enlightenment; a scholar, a wise guide

(For more on archetypes, read Joseph Campbell's seminal text, *The Hero With a Thousand Faces* (1949); works by Carl Jung; and *The Hero and The Outlaw* by Margaret Mark and Carol S. Pearson [New York: McGraw-Hall, 2001].)

COMPLEMENTS

Imagine you are two people—two opposites or a substantial duo. Famous business collaborators include Larry Page and Sergey Brin, Steve Jobs and Steve Wozniak, as well as artistic collaborators such as Vladimir Stenberg and Georgii Stenberg or Gilbert and George or Christo and Jeanne-Claude or Jake and Dinos Chapman. (There are celebrity duos, as well, such as eccentric magicians Penn and Teller, and classic comedians/actors, Abbott and Costello; Laurel and Hardy; and George Burns and Gracie Allen.) Could there be something in a pairing of your own invention (or a real pair of others you know of) that helps you realize or identify your own strengths?

Or think of it another way: Can you imagine mismatched pairs or adversarial pairs? Could a mismatch help you pinpoint your strengths?

Dualism is a theory of opposing concepts. People can have dual natures as well. Can you use contrasting, complementary principles—or opposite sides, elements, extremes, concepts, resonances, or themes to define yourself?

- Wildness and refinement
- Industrial and handmade
- Order and chaos
- Inferno and utopia
- Real and ideal
- Consonant and dissonant
- Unbridled and controlled
- Man and machine
- Human and beast
- Yin and Yang

ASSOCIATIONS

What are the important pieces that differentiate you? Choosing a positive association to define you could be a solution, or could be a springboard for further investigation.

Dr. Steven Doloff, Professor of Humanities and Media Studies at Pratt, advises:

"A brand is either a semiotic vehicle or a destination. If it's a vehicle, it's designed to visually and/or verbally direct your audience to some generally positive idea, feeling, or attitude with which you want to be associated. (Think Sunshine Bakers.) If it's a destination, it's designed to make your audience formulate for themselves your virtues by experiencing your product or service. (Think Smuckers Jam.) So in choosing a personal brand, ask yourself this question: Do you initially want to project a positive association, or do you want to create a mystery?"

Could sunshine represent you? Could a creature represent you? How about an element, such as wind or fire? How about a structure, either man-made or natural? A positive association—idea, feeling, or attitude—can act to represent you. For example, your audience will infer meaning from the use of a specific object you use to represent yourself.

If you use a walrus as your logo symbol, that walrus says something about you. If you use a cat as your logo symbol, that communicates something different than a walrus. If you design your name in English Copperplate Script, that says something quite different than designing your name in Futura. There are connotative as well as denotative levels of meaning.

Ethical Virtues

In the Arena Chapel (Cappella degli Scrovegni), Padua, Italy, there are magnificent frescoes by Giotto. In addition to the well-known frescoes, there are fourteen individual figures of seven virtues and seven vices. There are three theological virtues (Hope, Faith and Charity) and four classical virtues (Justice, Wisdom, Fortitude, and Temperance), as well as the vices (Despair, Infidelity, Envy, Injustice, Folly, Inconstancy, and Anger).

These imaginative incarnations can spark thinking about how something such as a virtue or vice can represent one creatively. Giotto depicts the vice of envy as a person with a serpent tongue that comes out of his mouth and bites him on the head. Although most of us would not want to identify ourselves with a vice, these concepts provide creative fodder.

Perhaps thinking about yourself in terms of ethical virtues will help determine your strengths. Professionally, ethical virtues would be those acquired attributes that constitute your character and enable you to design or write effectively.

Activity	Virtue
Entertaining ideas fairly	Evenhanded
Contemplating another's point of view	Tolerant
Faithfulness to reason or critical thinking	Rational
Considering possibilities	Flexible
Knowing one's limits	Humble
Rugged individualism	Authentic
Standing up for others or one's convictions	Courageous

Demonstration

In advertising, a demonstration is a display of how a product or service functions, and it usually provides evidence or proof of the brand's soundness. Since we get to observe a product or service in action, a demonstration provides useful information.

First and foremost, your personal brand identity is a demonstration of your design and copywriting skills. In a more literal fashion, you could demonstrate other skills by posting your working sketches or methodology on a blog, social site, or your website.

ORAL PRESENTATION TOOL

We all know writing or sketching can lead to an idea. Talking about the brand identity problem can lead to ideas and identifying insights as well.

Presenting or explaining your design problem to someone unfamiliar with it will force you to organize and articulate your thoughts, which might lead to a better understanding of the problem and ultimately to an insight or idea.

One method for making discoveries, whether to find a positive association or any insight, is to present this visual/verbal identity problem to someone else using the oral presentation tool.

ORAL PRESENTATION TOOL TECHNIQUE

1. Find a listener. This person should not attempt to help you solve the problem or even make any comments. If no one is available, use a tape recorder. You will need to actively listen to what you say for a possible key insight.

2. Present an overview of the problem. Then explain it in more detail. The listener should focus on you, and may nod to encourage you to keep speaking, but refrain from commenting so as not to interrupt your stream of thoughts. (Or ask the person to take notes, which you could use as jump-starts).

3. If this process has not yet stimulated an insight from which you can develop an idea, go to Step 4.

4. Once you finish speaking, the listener is free to ask questions—questions to clarify points or questions based on what you have presented. If the person has been attentive, then he or she may have some pointed questions that can aid in focusing your thinking.

> **"YOU EXPRESS YOURSELF ALL THE TIME, IN A VARIETY OF WAYS."**
> LINDA BRESKIN, PH.D. IN PSYCHOLOGY

THE QUEST OR "WHAT'S MY STYLE?"

One of the most often asked questions by aspiring designers is, "Do I need to have a style to be a designer?" This concern of many may have to do with our human nature, with our perennial quest for identity. Integral to the arts is the quest—the search for the true self, the adventurous expedition that helps us define who we are. Many are attracted to the study of psychology for the same reason. (And, it is fair to say, many designers and copywriters are naturally good at finding psychological insights into target audiences.)

In order to develop an authentic style, many start by imitating artists, illustrators, designers, or writers whose work they admire. Others imitate beloved genres. (Think of all the kids who start by drawing from comic books or by writing fan fiction.)

A discussion of style is complex. Is it a deviation from the pedestrian? Does it always have to be unique? Does it carry the meaning of the culture or carry the zeitgeist with it?

Designers and copywriters do *not* need to exhibit a style in their work—their work needs to be created for specific brands or groups based on communication objectives. Yes, there are some designers whose work is instantly recognizable, but that is not a requirement. Illustrators do have styles, but sometimes more than one.

Your brand identity should have a look and feel, or style, or some deliberate point of view. That style will communicate on a connotative level, whether you intend it or not. It's best to make sure you know what you're communicating. Apart from the denoted meanings of the words you use and the images you create, the formal components, the visualization and construction of a design or the specific construction of a sentence or paragraph, imply meaning. The constructive components of the work are inseparable from expressive qualities that ultimately refer back to the designer or writer.

Often a style is an outward visual expression that sets one apart from others, whether it's manifested in a personal brand identity, typography, tweets, or one's fashion. That is "style" (the look and feel of your brand identity) as opposed to "content" (your portfolio of work). For example, opera singer Maria Callas thought her distinctive fashion style was an important part of her persona. In order for her fashion style to indeed be a style, it had to stand apart from other opera stars.

In his famous essay, "Style," first published as part of a collection of essays in *Anthropology Today* in 1953, Meyer Schapiro wrote:

"By style is meant the constant form—and sometimes the constant elements, qualities, and expression—in the art of an individual or a group." Schapiro goes on: "But the style is, above all, a system of forms with a quality and a meaningful expression through which the personality of the artist and the broad outlook of a group are visible. It is also a vehicle of expression within the group, communicating and fixing certain values of religious, social, and moral life through the emotional suggestiveness of forms."

Here's a way to formulate it:

Authentic voice + personal vision = STYLE

"**WHENEVER** SPEECH OR MOVEMENT OR BEHAVIOR OR OBJECTS EXHIBIT A CERTAIN DEVIATION FROM THE MOST DIRECT, USEFUL, INSENSIBLE MODE OF EXPRESSION OR BEING IN THE WORLD, WE MAY LOOK AT THEM AS HAVING A 'STYLE,' AND BEING BOTH AUTONOMOUS AND EXEMPLARY."
SUSAN SONTAG, AMERICAN PHILOSOPHER, THEORIST, AUTHOR, AND ART CRITIC

Evaluating your Premise

- Tell people your brand personality. Ask them what they think.
- Ask them if they believe your core personality is truly authentic to you.
- Does it inspire interest? Generate enthusiasm?
- Does it deviate from the competition?
- Is your strategy based on an insight into you and your target audience?
- Can you own it? Could it be a platform?
- Does it tell a big story about you?
- Could the story be told in pieces across media?
- Will people connect with it? Will it resonate?
- Is it flexible?

Personal Projects

When you're looking for employment as a creative professional, you're trying to figure out what a prospective employer would like to see in your portfolio. Often a portfolio consists of work created for clients as well as projects created in a university or portfolio program. Many creative directors refer to some student work as "cookie cutter" projects—meaning, everyone has them. It's best to omit them from your portfolio.

Rarely do people include self-assigned projects in their portfolio. However, including personal design or writing projects can help a potential employer see your personal best and your particular vision. The act of creating those projects can help you realize what your strengths are, if you have a focus, and what's unique about your aesthetic vision.

Many designers create work that is private by design, including Seymour Chwast (sculpture), Jessica Hische (Daily Drop Cap), Jennifer Morla (paintings and sculptures), and Paula Scher (paintings), among many others. When you're solving design assignments in college or for a client, it's difficult to focus on what you find fascinating. Graphic artist Laura Alejo (www.lauraalejo.com) advises that a "very important note for new professionals is to always have a personal project to work on. Either by yourself or with a group, work on ideas, techniques that intrigue you. These projects will end up being your best calling card."

PERSONAL PROJECT PLATFORMS

Self-initiated projects are very useful:

- Explore your thoughts about design, image making or typography
- Tap into your artistry (creating things by hand, paper engineering, hand-lettering, book arts, silkscreen, letterpress, special bindings, etc.)
- Try new methods of visualization or media
- Work without worrying about the watchful eyes of instructors or creative directors or clients
- Collaborate with other designers, illustrators and writers
- Work unconventionally

"FIND ONE THING YOU'RE REALLY PASSIONATE ABOUT THAT IS VERY SPECIFIC AND UNIQUE. CREATE A TUMBLR, A BLOG OR A PINTEREST PAGE ABOUT IT. BUT YOU HAVE TO MAKE SURE IT'S SPECIFIC AND UNIQUE. FOR EXAMPLE, 'NORWEGIAN FOLKLORE MUSIC' RATHER THAN 'MUSIC,' '80S CUSTOM MADE SNEAKERS' RATHER THAN 'SHOES.' SPECIFICITY MAKES PEOPLE REMEMBER YOU. THE GENERIC IS ALWAYS FORGETTABLE."

ALESSANDRA LARIU, CO-FOUNDER OF SHESAYS (www.weareshesays.com)

INTERVIEW WITH DANY LENNON
FOUNDER/PRESIDENT, THE CREATIVE REGISTER

Q: *What is it about someone's visual and verbal presentation that makes you think, "I've got to represent this creative"?*

"It is a feeling, guttural and believable. It is also about chemistry, shared vision, shared principles and values, and just honestly an instinctive respect for each other. It is usually a seamless event, if right. The person and the work are 'one' as far as I am concerned. I do not separate them. They both equally have to pass the litmus test, which combines both their diverse and visionary creative skill sets with their humanitarian skill sets—equally! Another seamless event. There is no perfect solution, however. Everything is subjective, for the creative and for myself. We kid ourselves that we can be objective, but human instinct is such that we fight objectivity daily, and that is innate. But so far, this methodology and belief system has worked well for me, and the beauty of it is, it is part of the evolutionary process, so therefore adaptable to progress!"

Q: *What do you wish aspiring creatives knew about building their personal identities?*

"Know what 'your' brand is. The majority of people do not. When asked, they repeat what they feel, or what they have done. But brand identity is a lot more complex than what you feel or have done; it is in fact how you think! You own that.

Then, how you project what you are thinking. You own that too. Now define it with clarity and simplicity so everyone else can hear and understand what you are thinking and have something to truly believe in."

Q: *After years of placing junior and senior talent, what do you think creative directors are looking for in how people conceive, write, and design their visual and verbal identities?*

"Honesty, breadth, and reveal. Being able to do all that is not an easy task. It requires an ability to understand the past, the present and the future. And how you fit into that. How you perceive it through your work, your verbal communication, your presentational capabilities, and through your ability to expose your talents honestly. That means demonstrating what you have done, what you can do, what you want to do, and what you might be able to do. The ability also to recognize your weaknesses as much as your strengths is equally imperative. The honesty of knowing who you are and what might make you better. Revealing every part of you, not only proven but also maybe unproven. This can be revealed through work you have not even done yourself; instead work you admire, people you admire, or ideas that haven't yet come to fruition. Strangely enough, you can represent yourself not only through your own achievements, but through recognizing other people's achievements that inspire you to be better and to reach for a higher bar. Then there is the absolute necessity and that is 'the curious mind.' There is nothing more alluring than that. Curiosity reveals itself through the ability to ask, inquire, and absorb. So to question is as a much a gift as it is to answer. And finding a way to do all the above will, in my mind, give a Creative Director more to think about than the next person."

Prompts

CHOOSE FOUR NOUNS TO REPRESENT YOU, SUCH AS A TREE, BEAR, PINEAPPLE OR TRUMPET. SKETCH OR DESIGN THEM AND PLACE THEM IN HIERARCHICAL ORDER.

CASTING: WHO WOULD PLAY YOU IN A BIOGRAPHICAL MOVIE ABOUT YOUR LIFE? ASK YOURSELF AND YOUR CLOSEST FRIEND TO PICK THE ACTOR WHO COULD BEST PORTRAY YOU. COMPARE RESULTS. (MOST PEOPLE PICK SOMEONE WHO THEY THINK LOOKS LIKE THEM, ONLY BETTER. THEIR FRIENDS PICK SOMEONE WHO PLAYS CHARACTERS WITH A SIMILAR PERSONALITY.)

— STEPHEN T. HALL, PROFESSOR OF ADVERTISING, SAVANNAH COLLEGE OF ART AND DESIGN

HERE'S A TIMELINE. FILL IT IN WITH YOUR CAREER/LIFE.

Shakespeare's Hamlet disguises his true emotional state, pretending to be crazy, in his quest to seek revenge for his father's murder—only to find that he has disguised himself from his own understanding to the extent that he cannot take the actions that he wants and needs to take:

> "What is a man,/if his chief good and market of his time/be but to sleep and feed? A beast, no more... I do not know/why yet I live to say, 'this thing's to do,'/sith I have cause, and will, and strength, and means/to do't."

In *Twelfth Night*, Shakespeare's Viola disguises her true physical state by dressing in man's clothing and falls in love with the Duke she is serving—only to find that the Duke insists on using Viola to court another woman on his behalf. The result for Viola seems to be a profound and dangerous frustration. She tells the Duke:

> My father had a daughter loved a man/as it might be perhaps, were I a woman/I should love your lordship."

When the Duke asks, "And what's her history?" Viola replies:

> "A blank, my lord. She never told her love,/But let concealment, like a worm i' th' bud,/feed on her damask cheek. She pined in thought;/... smiling at grief.

"Write a verse or a prose poem about a real or imagined situation in which you disguised yourself only to arrive at unlooked-for consequences."

—Richard Nochimson, Ph.D., Professor of English, Yeshiva University

CIRCLE ALL THE SKILLS YOU POSSESS IN ONE COLOR MARKER AND ALL THE SKILLS YOU ASPIRE TO POSSESS IN ANOTHER COLOR MARKER.

ARTICULATE A PROBLEM.

FIND AN INSIGHT.

SOLVE COMMUNICATION PROBLEMS.

DEVELOP A VISUAL SOLUTION TO A DESIGN PROBLEM.

CONSTRUCT MEANINGFUL IMAGES.

UNDERSTAND AESTHETICS.

CONDUCT RESEARCH.

ANALYZE.

UNDERSTAND CULTURAL CONTEXTS.

WRITE CODE.

CREATE UNIQUE COLOR PALETTES.

PROTOTYPE.

UTILIZE A VARIETY OF TOOLS.

BECOME FAMILIAR WITH A BUNCH OF WELL-DESIGNED TYPEFACES.

EXPLORE NEW MEDIA.

UTILIZE TECHNOLOGY.

THINK CREATIVELY.

BE FLEXIBLE.

BE RECEPTIVE.

CRITIQUE MY OWN WORK.

UNDERSTAND ISSUES OF SUSTAINABILITY.

BE A TEAM PLAYER.

FUNCTION ON AN INTERDISCIPLINARY TEAM.

CONSTRUCT A RATIONALE.

USE TEXTURES AND PATTERNS CREATIVELY.

DETERMINE YOUR "WHY"—NOT "WHAT" YOU ARE OR "HOW" YOU DO IT, BUT THE REASON YOU DO WHAT YOU DO. THIS "WHY"—THE DRIVING FORCE THAT MAKES YOU TICK—SHOULD BE THE CORE OF YOUR PERSONAL BRAND.

(FOLLOW-UP STEPS FOR THOSE WHO HAVE DIFFICULTY ARTICULATING THEIR "WHY": DESCRIBE THE VERY FIRST TIME YOU CONSCIOUSLY RECOGNIZED YOU WANTED TO BE A DESIGNER. RECALLING YOUR EMOTIONS FROM THAT EXPERIENCE, EXPLAIN WHY YOU WERE DRAWN TO DESIGN. NOW EXPLAIN WHAT IT IS ABOUT DESIGN THAT MAKES YOU EXCITED TO WAKE UP EVERY MORNING AND DESIGN.)

—**DREW DAVIES, OWNER, OXIDE DESIGN CO.**

WHAT GIVES YOUR LIFE MEANING? WHAT GIVES YOUR CAREER MEANING? EXPLAIN IN WORDS OR SKETCHES.

MAKE A LIST OF THOSE PEOPLE WHOSE PERSONAL VISION YOU ADMIRE. CAN YOU ARTICULATE EACH PERSON'S ARTISTIC VISION? LIST EVERYONE'S CHARACTERISTICS AND QUALITIES THAT YOU ADMIRE ABOUT THEM. SKETCH OR WRITE ABOUT SOME OF THE ONES YOU THINK RELATE TO YOURSELF.

YOUR PERSONAL LIFE MAP: A PERSONAL LIFE MAP IS A MAP THAT IS BASED UPON PLACES TO WHICH YOU HAVE TRAVELLED OVER THE COURSE OF YOUR LIFETIME. ALTHOUGH YOU CAN CREATE A PERSONAL MAP BASED UPON YOUR DAILY ACTIVITIES AND ROUTES, HERE THE TASK IS TO MAP YOUR LIFE'S MAJOR TRAVELS BEYOND HOME, WORK AND SCHOOL. DOES YOUR LIFE MAP EXPLODE LIKE FIREWORKS OR IS IT FOCUSED? IN THE FUTURE, HOW DO YOU WISH TO CHANGE YOUR LIFE MAP?

—SUZANNE BOUSQUET, PH.D. IN COGNITIVE PSYCHOLOGY, DEAN, COLLEGE OF HUMANITIES AND SOCIAL SCIENCES, KEAN UNIVERSITY

CHANGE SOMETHING ABOUT THE WORLD.

REPAIR THE WORLD.

IF YOU WERE AN INTERACTIVE HOLOGRAM, WHAT WOULD YOU BE?

DEVELOP A REALITY SHOW ABOUT YOU.

WRITE YOUR OWN BIRTH ANNOUNCEMENT.

> LOOK BACK AS IF YOU WERE AT THE END OF YOUR LIFE, AND WRITE THE OBITUARY YOU WOULD WANT PUBLISHED ABOUT YOU, YOUR LIFE AND YOUR WORK.
>
> —MEGAN LANE PATRICK, CONTENT DIRECTOR, HOW MAGAZINE

CONCEIVE AN APPUMENTARY (APP + DOCUMENTARY): THIS PARTICULAR APP HIGHLIGHTS PIVOTAL MOMENTS IN YOUR LIFE AND CAREER, STREAMS YOUR MUSIC AND OFFERS AN INTERACTIVE APPROACH TO YOUR STORY UNLIKE ANYTHING WE HAVE SEEN BEFORE.

MAKE UP A DREAM ABOUT A LIFE CONFLICT YOU FACE.

—JILL BELLINSON, PH.D., PSYCHOLOGIST

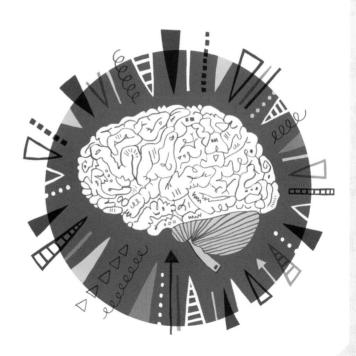

WHAT ARE THE MOST OFTEN REPEATED EXPRESSIONS HEARD ABOUT YOUR PROFESSION? WHAT'S YOUR MANTRA?

YOUR SOCIAL WORLD: CREATE A "SOCIOGRAM" (A GRAPHIC REPRESENTATION OF SOCIAL LINKS THAT PLOTS YOUR INTERPERSONAL RELATIONSHIPS). PUT YOURSELF IN THE MIDDLE, ADD CONNECTIONS BETWEEN YOU AND YOUR FAMILY, YOU AND YOUR FRIENDS, YOU AND YOUR CO-WORKERS. WHAT IS THE MOST IMPORTANT PART OF YOUR SOCIOGRAM? WHAT IS THE MOST COMPLICATED PART? WHAT IS THE MOST AESTHETICALLY PLEASING PART? IS IT A TANGLED SOCIOGRAM OR DO YOU KEEP DIFFERENT SPHERES OF YOUR LIFE SEPARATE?

—SUZANNE BOUSQUET, PH.D. IN COGNITIVE PSYCHOLOGY, DEAN, COLLEGE OF HUMANITIES AND SOCIAL SCIENCES, KEAN UNIVERSITY

STATE TWO FACTS ABOUT YOUR AREA OF EXPERTISE. INTERPRET ONE FACT IN A NEW WAY.

1.

2.

LIST THREE OF YOUR STRENGTHS. WHAT IS THE MOST UNIQUE STRENGTH YOU POSSESS?

1

2

3

WHAT MAKES YOU DIFFERENT? WHAT WOULD YOU BRING TO THE TABLE? WHAT CAN YOU OFFER A STUDIO OR AGENCY?

OUTLINE A FOUR-STEP PROCESS FOR WHAT YOU DO. IMAGINE IT IN A WAY THAT HAS NOT YET BEEN STATED OR COIN A NEW TERM FOR IT.

1.

2.

3.

4.

IN YOUR FIELD, DESCRIBE A RENEGADE. WHAT ARE THE POINTS OF DIFFERENCE BETWEEN A RENEGADE AND A CONVENTIONAL EXPERT?

DRAW YOUR FAVORITE HIDING PLACE.

DESCRIBE OR DRAW THE "YOU" NOBODY SHOULD EVER KNOW OR SEE.

DESCRIBE OR DRAW THE "YOU" PEOPLE ENJOY OR VALUE.

YOUR T-SHIRT READS: "I WANT TO…

YOUR T-SHIRT READS: I ASPIRE TO…

CHAPTER TWO
VERBAL IDENTITY

What's In A Name?

Call me Ishmael.

Other than an iconic photo of you, nothing says *you* like your name.

Apparently Bob Dylan didn't think his given name, Robert Zimmerman, had the right cachet for a music career. Sean John Combs has certainly had his share of names. Some find one name to be all they need.

What's in a name? If you're a James, what's the difference if you use Jim or James or Jimmy or Jimbo? Jimmy the Kid, perhaps?

Once you decide upon how your name will be cast, stick with it. Use it across media, for your résumé, domain, email and social media. There are differing opinions on using a less-than-professional sounding name. One could make a case for memorability over dogmatism. Though you could use a variety of nicknames as your theme, the bottom line is to keep your name system consistent so that people can find you and identify you.

"**JUST LIKE** BRANDS MUST COMPETE WITH OTHERS IN THEIR CATEGORIES TO BREAK THROUGH THE CLUTTERED CONSUMER MARKETPLACE, PROFESSIONALS MUST BREAK THROUGH THE COMPETITION AND GENERAL INDUSTRY NOISE TO LAND GREAT JOBS.

THE KEY TO STANDING OUT IS KNOWING WHAT YOU HAVE TO OFFER THAT IS SPECIAL AND UNIQUE—THEN MAKING SURE EVERY TOUCH POINT OF YOUR BRAND CONVEYS THIS UNIQUE SELLING PROPOSITION OR "USP."

ONCE YOU FIGURE OUT YOUR USP, BOIL IT DOWN TO ONE STATEMENT SO SHORT AND SWEET IT COULD FIT ON A BADGE PINNED TO YOUR LAPEL.

THIS IS YOUR PROFESSIONAL BRAND POSITIONING AND YOUR GUIDE TO CREATING THE PLETHORA OF TOUCH POINTS THAT WILL BRING TO LIFE WHO YOU ARE AND HELP YOU STAND OUT VS. THE COMPETITION.

FROM YOUR ELEVATOR PITCH TO YOUR PROFESSIONAL WEBSITE, EVERY VEHICLE SHOULD BRING YOUR BRAND POSITIONING TO LIFE. WITH A CLEAR, SINGLE-MINDED POSITIONING, YOU'LL DIFFERENTIATE FROM YOUR PEERS AND HAVE A MEMORABLE IMPACT ON PROFESSIONALS IN YOUR INDUSTRY."

—KRISTEN CAMPOLATTARO, BRAND STRATEGIST AND COMMUNICATIONS PROFESSOR AT COLUMBIA UNIVERSITY

LIBERATING YOUR INNER WRITER

Before you attempt to write mindfully, here are some beneficial exercises to help you free your thoughts and writing.

AUTOMATIC ART AND WRITING

One of the premises of spontaneous art or writing is that it allows access to your subconscious and liberates you from inhibitions. You create images or write without concerns regarding conventions, aesthetics, composition, and intention. There are no restrictions on content, and you are not governed by the constraints of an assignment. Performing an automatic art exercise also might free you to write. If you are a visual artist, carrying out the art exercise first is a good warm-up before doing the automatic writing.

Spontaneous Art Process

Enjoy the process without concerning yourself with an end product or whether you finish anything. Choose any preferred art medium and approach: traditional or nontraditional, nonrepresentational, abstract or representational.

- Start making art
- Keep working
- Move from surface to surface or medium to medium, as you like.

If you're not sure which subject matter or techniques to explore, choose one of the following:

Subject Matter
- Still life
- Cityscapes, landscapes, interiors
- Emotions
- Nonrepresentational patterns or textures

Techniques/Media
- Collage
- Photomontage
- Rubbings/Blottings
- Automatic Drawing: to draw automatically you must not deliberate on the drawing itself but allow yourself to draw in a stream of consciousness. Automatic drawing works well using conventional media or a digital tablet with digital pen or stylus. A mouse isn't the best tool for this exercise.
- Doodling: a form of automatic drawing
- Modeling clay (conventional material or air-dry modeling material, such as Crayola® Model Magic®, works well for automatic or spontaneous clay modeling)
- Painting: India ink on large sheets of paper or on blank paper towels works well for this process. Try placing large sheets of paper on the floor rather than on a tabletop or easel. Using a floor surface allows you to paint using arm movements (think Jackson Pollock) as opposed to wrist movements.

(See Chapter 5, Resources, for more visualization techniques.)

Spontaneous Writing Process

There are different spontaneous writing techniques. Surrealist André Breton advocated the following in his First Surrealist Manifesto:

"**Write quickly with no preconceived subject, so quickly that you retain nothing and are not tempted to re-read. The first sentence will come by itself, since it is true that each second there exists a sentence foreign to our conscious thoughts, which asks only to be brought out in to the open.**"

Writer Jack Kerouac, in "The Essentials of Spontaneous Prose," compared his method of spontaneous writing to jazz—writing in an undisturbed flow, without concern for "selectivity."

- Assume a receptive and relaxed state of mind.
- Focus on a familiar subject in the present or from memory.
- Write without interruption. (If you stop after a few sentences, start the next sentence randomly with any letter and continue from there.)
- Don't worry about usage or grammar.
- Don't give thought to style, convention or form.
- Move freely from thought to thought. Don't fret about making sense.
- Enjoy the process without concerning yourself with an end product or whether you finish anything.
- Write until the uninterrupted flow is satisfied. (You can always start fresh.)

> "If you have any young friends who aspire to become writers, the second greatest favor you can do them is to present them with copies of *The Elements of Style.* The first greatest, of course, is to shoot them now, while they're happy."
> —Dorothy Parker

Telling Your Story

What's your story? The raw material is about you—who you are, what you've done, what your strengths are, where you hope to work and more. No formal research is necessary, though much analysis is required.

To write an elevator pitch or "about me" statement or Twitter profile, use writing as a discovery process. In the course of free writing, a core message may appear somewhere in the body of the written content. Writing also will help you find a distinguishing voice (a quality that makes the writing unique or specifically yours), or a point of view (the writer's attitude or the perspective from which the writer recounts a narrative or presents the information).

> "The most valuable of all talents is that of never using two words when one will do."
> —Thomas Jefferson

> "**Vigorous writing is concise. A sentence should contain no unnecessary words, a paragraph no unnecessary sentences, for the same reason that a drawing should have no unnecessary lines and a machine no unnecessary parts. This requires not that the writer make all his sentences short, or that he avoid all detail and treat his subjects only in outline, but that every word tell."**
> —William Strunk Jr., *The Elements of Style*

Drawing upon your story's raw material, which contains many facts of your life, you have to craft a central message. To determine your story's premise, begin with these tasks:

- Conceive a core message by synthesizing experiences and expertise (academic studies, accomplishments, sequences of events) into a theme or premise.
- Omit. What you take out is as important as what you leave in.
- Show, don't tell. Use action to show. Resist explaining. (If you're funny, be funny. Don't say you're funny. If you want the readers to find something amusing, make them feel amused.)
- State it clearly and memorably.
- Specificity helps people get an idea of which assets you will bring to the job. Conversely, using superlatives and making general statements isn't useful. For example, writing "I am the greatest designer of my generation" isn't as useful (or believable) as stating specifically what makes you exceptional.
- Consider the payoff. Is there a payoff to the employer in how you define yourself? For example, if you characterize yourself as an *enfant terrible*, you will want to make sure it translates to mean that your work is edgy or exciting, and not that you'll embarrass the employer by doing outrageous things.

(In the prompts section of Chapter 1, you can create a timeline of your life (see page 29), that cites watershed moments. Then you can make another life map to delineate your attributes across the timeline. This will help you edit.)

> **Writing Objectives**
>
> Extract your story's premise through selection, looking for an insight.
> Make it pithy. Eliminate extraneous material but retain the fabric of your personal and professional DNA. Also edit for repetitiveness.
>
> Write genuinely and specifically—your statement is about you, not suitable for anyone else. If your competition can insert her name into your statement, then it's too broad or generic.

THE PITCH

You are crafting a pitch to presell your capabilities. Jamesian and other styles of prose aside, the requisite writing form to craft such a short piece as this (or craft *bon mots* for social media) is based on *The Elements of Style* by Strunk and White, with similar form advocated by writers such as Ernest Hemingway and Stephen King.

"Do not overwrite," is the dictum. "Omit needless words," instructs *The Elements of Style*.

Advocating a minimalist form doesn't mean the thoughts you produce should be minimal or dull. To illustrate: "Get off your sofa and run" doesn't have the same impact as "Just Do It."

How you craft a few select words counts.

Pointer: Many people feel the need to offer too much information. They provide lots of backstory because they think the audience won't understand what they're saying unless the audience hears and knows everything. With insight into what the key message ought to be, the few sentences you craft should be rich enough to illuminate your backstory.

ADVICE FROM THE KANSAS CITY STAR STYLEBOOK

Below are excerpts from *The Kansas City Star* stylebook, which Ernest Hemingway once credited with containing "the best rules I ever learned for the business of writing."

"USE SHORT SENTENCES. USE SHORT FIRST PARAGRAPHS. USE VIGOROUS ENGLISH. BE POSITIVE, NOT NEGATIVE."

"NEVER USE OLD SLANG."

"ELIMINATE EVERY SUPERFLUOUS WORD."

Guidelines for Writing the Pitch

Omit any element—event, word, fact, reference—that does not contribute to what best presents you. Unless you're a professional or proficient writer, follow these general mechanics guidelines:

- Write short complete sentences containing a subject, predicate, and verb. (The subject is the one performing the action and the verb is the action.) As Stephen King wrote in *On Writing: A Memoir of the Craft*, "Take any noun, put it with any verb, and you have a sentence. It never fails."
- Use action verbs.
- Write in the active voice, not in the passive voice.
- Average fewer than twenty words per sentence. (Design-wise, twelve words is a good line length on a website.)
- Start the sentence with a capital letter and end the sentence with a period.
- Use adjectives and adverbs sparingly. Avoid superlatives. (Rather than saying you're the "best," give an example of what makes you best.)
- Avoid redundancy.
- Cut as many words as possible while retaining meaning.
- Convey a precise meaning with each word.
- Draw in the reader with the first sentence.
- Leave an impression with the last sentence.
- Use everyday language.
- Avoid clichés.
- Spellcheck.

> "I FORGET WHO STARTED THE NOTION OF MY WRITING A SERIES OF ANGLO-INDIAN TALES... THEY WERE ORIGINALLY MUCH LONGER THAN WHEN THEY APPEARED, BUT THE SHORTENING OF THEM, FIRST TO MY OWN FANCY AFTER RAPTUROUS RE-READINGS, AND NEXT TO THE SPACE AVAILABLE, TAUGHT ME THAT A TALE FROM WHICH PIECES HAVE BEEN RAKED OUT IS LIKE A FIRE THAT HAS BEEN POKED. ONE DOES NOT KNOW THAT THE OPERATION HAS BEEN PERFORMED, BUT EVERYONE FEELS THE EFFECT."
> —From *Something of Myself* by Rudyard Kipling

Elevator Speech

You have a couple of seconds—maybe three—to make a first impression on someone.

You know this is true because within a few seconds you, too, size up people. We all do. Therefore it's important to be prepared to clearly explain who you are, what you do, what you want and what you offer. If you've ever been in a situation where you stumbled over explaining what you do, then you can understand how crucial being prepared is to presenting and promoting yourself.

Of course, when you speak to someone, whatever you say shouldn't sound canned or rehearsed. You will need to craft your pitch well enough and rehearse it often enough that your spiel flows naturally and sounds conversational. And you'll want to be able to quickly tailor it to the specific listener. For example, you might pitch yourself differently to a design studio head than you would to an in-house design corporate executive or to your neighbor who knows someone in the business.

In the time that it takes to ride the elevator (say, thirty seconds or less), you should be able to deliver your pitch with time left for conversation. When you network at conferences and professional functions, you are afforded very little time to present yourself. Most people do not want to listen to a pitch for longer than thirty seconds. Most would prefer fifteen seconds. But if you rouse their interest, people might ask questions. And that's where those first two or three seconds come into play very strongly.

To make a good impression in those first two seconds, your opening line needs to be intriguing enough that someone would be inclined to ask you to explain further. Or so interesting that you'll keep the person's attention in order to say two more sentences.

If your opening line is concise and so intriguing that people will ask a question of you in return, that's ideal. That way, you've started a conversation with the other person rather than delivering a short monologue. If your story is authentic and personal, then it won't come off as an attempt at persuasion or sound conceited. It will be genuine.

What is the one thing you wish someone to know about you? What makes your story unique? Specifically, what can you offer an employer? A client? Anyone?

What qualifies you to work for a top studio or agency? As Kristen Campolattaro suggests, what is your unique selling proposition (USP)? That is a codified quality that differentiates you in a way that will make employers prefer you to your rivals.

Alternately, you may want to craft a very straightforward speech, for example, "I am a digital designer specializing in mobile web." This opening line states what you do but doesn't differentiate you. The second line could then act as the differentiator. However, remember that an elevator pitch is not a list of your skills or educational experiences. Those are listed on your *résumé*.

CRAFTING THE ELEVATOR PITCH

If you can state your premise in one sentence, that's a great start. In fact, if stated well, that could be the entire pitch. For example, my pitch is, "I am a designer who writes."

Craft a three-sentence pitch with the following objectives:

First sentence: Draw interest. Hook the listener with an attention-grabbing, active first sentence. The opening line leads to more, pointing to a fuller story.

Second sentence: Content. Engage the listener with content about yourself. Show; don't tell.

Third sentence: The payoff. What you can bring to the party—or—the essential takeaway message. The last line leaves an impression, like the ta-da! ending of a performance. What do you want to imprint on the listener?

After writing it, read it aloud. If any of it sounds contrived or not like something you would say conversationally, rewrite so it sounds genuine. If any of it trips you up when you say it aloud, rewrite.

A well-crafted elevator pitch also can act as your social media profile and LinkedIn profile.

Your objectives are:
- Tell your unique story.
- Have a hook—a premise that immediately grabs the listener's interest and makes him want to keep listening to you or engage in conversation with you.
- Communicate clearly, concisely.
- Tailor it to the audience.

Tools to Aid Crafting Your Verbal Brand

MAPPING TOOL TO AID WRITING

A mind map is a visual representation or diagram of the various ways themes, words, images or ideas can be related to one another. Mapping is a brainstorming and visual diagramming tool used to generate or develop an idea. It can be used to visualize and structure ideas and as an aid in study, organization and problem solving. There is a central key word or thought, and all other words, thoughts or visuals stem from and are linked to the central idea in a radius around that nucleus. A resulting visual map is a diagram that represents thoughts, words, information or images in a specific relational arrangement.

Types of Mind Maps

Mapping is a useful tool for the writing process, design process, brainstorming process, for exploring relationships among ideas or simply for thinking something through. You can approach mind mapping in two basic ways.

1) **Automatic mapping** relies heavily on the Surrealist strategy of spontaneous free association, avoiding conscious choices and allowing associations to flow freely.

2) **Deliberate mapping** relies more on the natural growth of associations, revealing the way your mind instinctively organizes or makes associations.

A mind map is a tangible representation of associations that may reveal an insight or lead to an idea. You can rearrange items to create a new beginning (central word or image), reorder subtopics (secondary items), sub-subtopics (tertiary items) and so on. You can remap based on a deeper understanding derived from the first go-round or based on something that occurred to you while mapping.

How to Create a Mind Map

Mapping software that offers templates, shuffling, notes, labels, cross-linking, and more is available. However, since the nature of the drawing process maximizes spontaneous mapping, doing it by hand may offer superior outcomes. Drawing your own map assures personalization and a natural flow of thoughts.

- Position an extra-large sheet of paper in landscape position.
- At the center of the page, your starting point, draw a key visual or write a key word, topic or theme.
- Starting with the central word or image, draw branches (using lines, arrows, etc.) in all directions, making as many associations as possible. Don't preconceive or judge. Write or draw freely.

Each subtopic should branch out from the major central topic. Then each subtopic or image should have sub-subtopic branches and so on. Seek relationships and generate branches among as many items as possible. Feel free to repeat items or to cross-link.

Spontaneous mapping draws upon the unconscious. Write or draw as quickly as possible without deliberating or editing. This type of mapping promotes nonlinear thinking. It can be the most random item or possibility that becomes a key to idea generation. Deliberate mapping utilizes long and careful thinking. As a complement, you could consider note taking—writing down some explanatory notes near the items or branches so that later, when you reexamine the map, you can more easily recall exactly what you were thinking.

Use Mapping for Your Elevator Speech

Crafting your pitch requires writing and revisions. You're concentrating on:

- Who you are
- What makes you singular
- What you can bring to the job

Start with a mind map. Either write a key word in the center of the page or draw a key image. The key word could be your goal, such as "web designer," or it could be your name or any word or image that will prompt mapping. Branch out spontaneously from that key word or image without thinking too much.

Using Lists to Craft a Pitch

- State your goals in a list.
- State your strengths and skills in a list.
- State what is unique about you. Perhaps you're very friendly, versatile, ethical, resourceful or you have a nimble mind. Anything that is distinctively you.

"REVIEW YOUR HAIR, CLOTHES, FURNITURE, FOOD AND THE CAR YOU DRIVE. YOU MADE BRAND CHOICES—DO THEY ACCURATELY REFLECT YOUR PERSONAL BRAND?"

STEVE LISKA, OWNER, LISKA + ASSOCIATES

Write the Opposite

- Write the most obvious, boring statement about yourself. Critique it. What makes it obvious? Boring? (Don't laugh. This exercise works to show what you should not write.)
- List all the qualities and skills—good and bad—that you do not possess. Then list the ones you do possess.
- Write an interesting story about yourself. Critique it. Cite exactly what makes it more interesting than the boring statement.

Expressing Your Individuality

Psychologist Linda Breskin, Ph.D., says, "You've expressed your individuality in many ways all your life. Now, it's a matter of putting it into words."

List ways you express your individuality. It could be the way you wear a hat or how you sign your e-mails, or the way you craft ligatures or your inspired color palettes. Hopefully, you'll be able to identify a bunch.

THE OPENING LINE

The opening line is the setup. It portends, leading to something more.

The opening line also suggests the overarching message, carrying your DNA.

Options for crafting the opener:

- It's best practice not to write the opening line first. Write your entire story in order to discover the hook, which you can pull from the fabric of the story.
- Some people begin with the end; with the payoff.
- Pose a question. What question does the listener want answered?
- State your promise.
- Juxtapose two facts.
- Use a metaphor.
- Look at your story from an unusual point of view. Try a new perspective on your story.
- Challenge your own notion of yourself.
- Reverse the listener's expectations.
- Be humorous.
- Create mystery.
- Build tension.
- Solve a problem.

Again, start by writing your entire story first. Revise. Wait a while. Revise. Sleep on it. Refine.

Résumé and Cover Letter

A résumé is a summary of your skills, education, and work experiences given to prospective employers. Often it is the first document that potential employers or creative recruiters see that represents you and your professional skills. Initially the best way to approach your résumé is as an information design project.

Gather and present information in a clear and interesting way. Your résumé is information design (clear information hierarchy) as well as a visual identity design (your distinctive brand) and a promotional design project (differentiates you and promotes your capabilities). The most important issues are visual hierarchy, unity, clear communication, readability, visual interest and impeccable typography.

"Substance over style is the rule for ALL résumés. Any special effects will dilute the gravitas and stature of the impression. You want people to concentrate on your accomplishments and your successes, not the curlicues of a font or unusual shades or contrast of colors," says Debbie Millman, president, Design at Sterling Brands, in an interview in Allison Cheston's article, "Will a Graphic Résumé Get You the Job? The Experts Respond," in *Forbes* magazine (http://www.forbes.com/sites/work-in-progress/2012/06/28/will-a-graphic-resume-get-you-the-job-the-experts-respond/).

A résumé should be neat, legible and well-designed. Design one for print as well as a downloadable PDF.

For students, it is important to include both design skills and technical skills. In addition, students can include work experience that is unrelated to the professional field because it demonstrates the ability to land and keep a job. You certainly want to include any design-related or copywriting experience, such as internships or freelance work. For designers with at least five years of experience, be sure to (briefly) include responsibilities, skills and client lists.

THE GOAL OF YOUR RÉSUMÉ

A résumé can take many forms, especially one made for a creative design or advertising professional. It provides standard information, but you can include whatever you want, in any form you want, as long as it works to inform the recipient, identify you and promote you. Conceivably, a résumé could be one sentence or a formatted paragraph, or it may take a more conventional form and content—whichever best reflects the mission of your brand identity.

Conventional Résumé Contents

Name
Contact: Email, Phone, Website, Social Media
Education (most recent information first)

Skills: Design and Technical
Experience: Design/Work (most recent information first)
Honors, Organizations, Extras

Sample Résumé Content

This section is only a guide for résumé content, not résumé design. Be sure to include complete contact information. Your phone, email and web address should be functional for at least a few months.

Name
Phone number
Email address
Web address

Objective: *If you want to include an objective, keep it succinct. (I'm not a fan of objective statements but if you must, make it pithy or witty.)*

   (Straightforward example:) Seeking a position as a (graphic designer; art director; copywriter)

Education: *List college and graduate degrees with most recent listed first. Include degree, date of degree, major and honors.*

   2017 BFA: Graphic Design, Robert Busch School of Design at Kean University

   2013–2017 Dean's List; Graduated Magna Cum Laude

Design Skills: *List design/copy/tech competencies.*

   Editorial Design, Branding, Web Design, Designing with Code

- *Don't exaggerate when listing your skills. Do not claim to be proficient in any area that you are not.*
- *List software and any front- or back-end developing.*
- *List fluency in any languages. Advertising agencies or design studios with global clients may be especially interested in a bilingual candidate.*

Experience *Start with your most recent position and include job titles. Very briefly describe your responsibilities. Use present tense for current jobs. Use past tense for past job experience. Include a client list when applicable.*

2015–present **The Design Studio at Kean University** | Design Intern
- Develop concepts and design with creative director based on creative briefs
- Work with clients and vendors
- Clients include: The College of Visual and Performing Arts at Kean University, Union County Park System, Liberty Hall Preservation, and The Community Food Bank of New Jersey

(Note: A bulleted list of sentence fragments does not take periods.)

2014–present **CVS Pharmacy** | Assistant Store Manager
- Responsibilities include employee scheduling, customer relations and quality control

2013–2014 **The United Way** | Volunteer Graphic Designer
- Collaborated with design director on idea generation and design

2012–2013 **Juno Studio** | Production Intern
- Digital prepress and preflight of designer's print files

Awards and Honors: *List all professional awards; this will demonstrate that your work has been recognized as outstanding. Simply list the year, organization and award title.*
- 2015 Gold Pencil/The One Club student competition
- 2015 Top 100/Art Directors Club National Portfolio Review
- 2014 CLIO award/student category

Professional Workshops: *List advanced course work, specialized training and workshops.*
- 2015 Philadelphia Art Directors Club Workshop: Motion Graphics
- 2014 HOW Design Conference Workshop: Handmade Typography
- 2013 HOW Design Conference Workshop: Responsive Web

COVER LETTER

A cover letter is an introductory business letter that accompanies a résumé, whether in an email window or printed. Brevity, clarity and proper form are vital.

Address the recipient as "Mr. or Ms. Last Name:" and spell it correctly. Do not use informal language as a salutation; for example, "Hey" or "Hi" is inappropriate. Use the personal title and last name followed by a colon. It is acceptable to use only the first name in the salutation (for example: Dear Jim:), if you know the person. "To Whom It May Concern" is a last resort if you don't know the specific recipient's name, but you should make an effort to find out the proper name. Call the firm or check the name online. Some firms prefer communication sent to the talent recruiter or human resources officer. Others prefer letters sent to the creative director. Find out or send the letter to both to play it safe; address the letters accordingly.

Do not repeat many facts contained in your accompanying résumé. Rather, include something not in your résumé, such as your unique qualities or what differentiates you. Explain what you specifically can bring to the studio or agency.

Résumé Tips

- Check spelling.
- Proofread several times.
- Be diligent about clarity of communication.
- Be concise. Brevity wins.
- Make it readable and legible.
- Use margins well. Margins present content.
- Don't use type: at such a small size it will be difficult to read.
- Create a master résumé that you can customize for specific career opportunities.

- For students and novices, keep the résumé to one page.
- Use a professional e-mail address with your name in it, such as betty_landa[at]gmail.com, not the one you might use for your friends, such as cutiepie[at]gmail.com, or a generic one, such as greatdesigner4all[at]gmail.com.

Keep the cover letter brief and to the point. Check your spelling and usage.

As a penultimate line in the letter, some candidates write, "I will call you next week to follow up." If you do, then call.

Unless requested, salary requirements are not included.

Use action verbs such as *demonstrated, delivered, attained, created, completed* and so on.

Conclude with a formal business letter closure such as "Sincerely yours," or "Yours truly."

Select quality paper for the cover letter and résumé.

Be prepared to upload a digital version of your cover letter and résumé, if required.

TWITTER

Your personal brand mission on Twitter is to do one of the following:

- Inform
- Entertain
- Promote
- Connect
- Do good
- Be discreet. (Don't post anything that would compromise your present or future.)
- Be positive, not negative.

TWITTER BIO

To write a Twitter bio, conceive the one statement you can make about yourself that hooks your listener's interest, making them curious to know more. At first, start writing with an extreme point of view, the more outrageous the better: odd combinations or juxtapositions, or two strengths juxtaposed or combined into an active statement.

Actor Simon Helberg's (@simonhelberg) Twitter bio is: "i act. i play music. i was born two years before my siamese twin… so annoying. and i have an autographed first edition of the Bible."

On Twitter, Lee Clow is Lee Clow's Beard, @leeclowsbeard: "Musings on advertising and facial topiary. Usually daily. Often dandruff-free."

Pete Jones, @pjones4, writes: "Group Creative Director @ KBS+P. Doing work on lots of stuff, plus this, that and the other thing we talked about…"

Next, write a straightforward bio statement. For example, Steven Brower, @StevenIanBrower, "designer/author/educator/musician."

Is there a way to mesh the two, the outlandish with the straightforward? For example, Margrethe Lauber, @profLauber, writes: "I teach art history and graphic design to impressionable (and sometimes brilliant and talented) young minds at a small ag/tech college in rural NYS."

Refine your statement.

Try it on your friends at the end of your e-mails and see if anyone notices.

> "I DON'T WANT TO KNOW YOU ARE DRUNK ON YOUR FRIEND'S BOAT, YOU HATE YOUR BOSS TODAY OR PROFANITY IS IN YOUR VOCABULARY. IF YOU POST IT ON FACEBOOK, EVERYBODY KNOWS, INCLUDING POTENTIAL EMPLOYERS. YOU ARE INSTANTLY TARNISHING YOUR BRAND."
> —JAIME LYNN PESCIA, ART DIRECTOR, DESIGNER, EDUCATOR

INTERVIEW WITH LAURENCE VINCENT

BIO: Laurence Vincent is the head of The Brand Studio at United Talent Agency, an innovative strategic branding consultancy. Over the past two decades, he has developed strategies for some of the world's most beloved brands, including CBS, Disney, Coca-Cola, Four Seasons Hotels, MasterCard, Microsoft, the NFL, Sony PlayStation, The Home Depot, and vitaminwater. He has written two books on branding, *Brand Real: How Smart Companies Live Their Brand Promise and Inspire Fierce Customer Loyalty* and *Legendary Brands: Unleashing the Power of Storytelling to Create a Winning Market Strategy*. He is also the author of *Mad Man's Creed*, a collection of poetry.

Q: *At The Brand Studio at United Talent Agency (UTA), you say storytelling is the root of every great brand. How does this strategy relate to personal brand building across media?*

I think Jonathan Gottschall got it right when he referred to humans as a "storytelling animal." You might argue that our penchant for stories is one of the qualities that differentiates us from other animals. It's how our brains work. We're born with it, and we celebrate this innate gift throughout our lives. Stories help us understand. Stories help us remember. Stories help us share.

When I say that storytelling is at the root of every great brand, what I really mean is that great brands channel into our storytelling mind.

When we think of these brands, we piece together a narrative. It's kind of magic. I'll give you an example. I read a piece in *The New York Times* about Tim Pawlenty, who was a possible running mate for Mitt Romney, the 2012 Republican presidential nominee. The story said that Pawlenty was a "Sam's Club Republican." Sam's Club is a big box retailer that promises quality brands at wholesale prices. The reference to Sam's Club was a clever way by campaign managers to position Pawlenty against other Republican candidates who have faced tough questions about their affluence. With a simple reference to the Sam's Club brand, Pawlenty's team told a story about their candidate.

Q: *How is a brand position different from a brand promise and how do they relate to personal branding?*

A position is simply a claim. It's a definitive statement that is meant to persuade you to think a certain way about a subject. Advertising and public relations rely on positioning because every advertisement and every PR campaign intends to plant an idea in your head. That's different from a promise. When I make a promise, I set an expectation. I commit myself to deliver a benefit to you. Brands make promises. In fact, a brand is a promise.

You will create a great personal brand if you focus on your promise—if you make it very clear what people should expect from you. That promise becomes your bar, and you'll want to deliver an experience that exceeds that bar every chance you get. In fact, as you age and develop, you want to raise the expectation. That's how you'll find growth.

The alternate path is to position yourself without a promise. You can make a lot of claims and consistently alter the way you're positioned to satisfy trends and the whims of opportunity. But if these positioning exercises set an expectation that you cannot fulfill, you'll have a reputation problem.

Q: *If you were to give a speed workshop in personal branding, what four matters would you emphasize?*

Passion and values—You can't build your personal brand without understanding what drives you. What are your passions? How do these relate to what matters to you? Where are the "hills that you're prepared to die on?" In other words, which of your values are most sacred?

Credibility—How much do people trust you, and what's the basis of that trust? Are you credible because you are always candid, honest and friendly, or are you credible because no one can do your job as well as you? Are you credible because you are trustworthy or because you are expert? Maybe both? When people want to grow their personal brand, much of their effort will be focused on strengthening and extending their credibility.

Voice—The voice inside your head is a story of who you are. It's always changing a little, but it's there. That story of who you are doesn't always connect with the story others would tell about you. To build a personal brand, you have to close the gap. In a perfect world, the story in your head about who you are matches the story others perceive about you. We close the gap by focusing on your narrative and how it affects your brand's voice.

Reflection—You can only build a great personal brand if you train yourself to listen and take time to reflect. We can get so caught up trying to succeed in our lives that we filter out the important feedback others and our environment provide. This is why companies hire branding consultants like me. The people inside the company are so close to the problem they lose perspective.

They need an outside point of view to help them evaluate where they are and what they need to change. If you're trying to build your personal brand, you need feedback, and you need time to step back and reflect on what you know about yourself and where you want to focus your energy to take your brand to the next level.

Q: *What are the keys to creating a memorable personal brand?*

Be credible. Be passionate. Be relevant. If you can master those three, your brand will be unstoppable.

INTERVIEW WITH ROB WALLACE
MANAGING PARTNER, STRATEGY, WALLACE CHURCH, INC.

BIO: Ask Rob Wallace what he does for a living and he'll tell you that he has the world's most engaging job. As managing partner of Wallace Church Inc., a Manhattan— and San Francisco—based brand identity strategy and package design consultancy, Rob works with some of the world's smartest and most successful consumer brand marketers.

Current Wallace Church clients include Procter & Gamble, Nestlé, Heinz, Pfizer, Dell and more than three dozen other fast-moving global consumer brand corporations of equal caliber.

Rob is among the Board of Directors and the chair of the Design Valuation Committee at the Design Management Institute, the world's leading design strategy consortium. He is among ten members of the Distinguished Faculty of the Path to Purchase Institute and a speaker at more than three dozen industry events across North America, Europe and Asia. He lectures annually at Columbia Business School and many other MBA programs.

Brand identity is not just Rob's job; it's his passion. Often referred to as "the thought-leader on design's return on investment," Rob sees his primary goal as proving that brand identity/package design is a marketer's single most effective tool.

When he's not traveling or entertaining with his wife and three adult daughters, Rob plays a wicked blues harmonica and a truly terrible game of golf.

Q: *If you were writing the bible for personal branding, what four points would you stress?*

Be Benefit Focused
Personal branding—that is, crafting yourself—is much like crafting an organization or shaping a product. Go beyond your background and expertise (your "product features") and recast your experience into how it helped to solve problems, build consensus, drive change and create value (the benefits you create through your experience). Then focus on how these benefits affected those you have worked with. Pride yourself not on your accomplishments, but on how they drove the success of others on your team and those that you mentor.

Be Curious
You can't be an expert at everything, but you can focus on a few areas and remain ever curious about everything else. People flock to those who can discern meaning from information. A curious person has many perspectives from which to draw that meaning. Read, write, contribute, analyze, share, grow.

Be Relevant
We live at a pace where change happens exponentially faster every day. What worked yesterday is often no

longer effective today. Keep pace. Stay informed. Challenge convention. Have a process and protocol but be flexible. Learn from those who adapt fastest. Embrace change.

Lastly and importantly, be real. One of the best pieces of advice on personal branding I've gotten came from Phil Duncan, VP Design of Procter & Gamble, when he said, "Be who you are, not who you think we want you to be". Great brands, like great people and great organizations, need to be a little polarizing. Being right for a very specific purpose means you can't be right for every purpose. Find your unique core, work from your strengths, be honest and you will live your brand.

Q: *How can one best differentiate oneself from the competition?*

Have a personal mission statement and a point of view. Take folks on a journey of where you started from, the mistakes you have made and what you learned from both these mistakes and your successes. Ask questions and listen hard. People will often tell you exactly what they want. Don't be afraid to be provocative. Poke holes in convention. Find out what people are really committed to.

Q: *What advice can you offer about writing one's elevator pitch?*

Like every effective piece of communication, your pitch needs to be a story. Build yours in chapters. Have a 10-second intro, a 10–15 second middle and a 5–10 second conclusion. Stop there and ask if people would like to hear more. If you are a good storyteller, chances are that you will have engaged them and they will want to stay engaged after the elevator ride.

Q: *What is your advice on using social media to promote oneself?*

Social media is just another way to tell your story, but here your story should be crafted in a way that allows the recipient to access it in his or her own way, determining how deep they want to go. To me, tweets can be a little A.D.D., a bit flippant. Short and frequent blogs may work more effectively. Networking platforms like LinkedIn, Experts.com and others are more like a springboard to connect person to person. Social media is a way to lure people in and encourage more engagement.

PROMPTS

INVENT FIVE DIFFERENT NAMES FOR YOURSELF: A STAGE NAME, AN ALTER EGO, A PEN NAME, A NICKNAME, A MUSIC INDUSTRY OR SPORTS PERSONA, OR WHATEVER YOU LIKE. WHICH TYPEFACES WOULD WORK FOR EACH? HAND-LETTERING?

WRITE A PRESS RELEASE ABOUT YOUR NEW PRODUCT LAUNCH. YOUR PRODUCT IS YOU.

—JAIME LYNN PESCIA, ART DIRECTOR, DESIGNER, EDUCATOR

WRITE ONE WORD IN THE CENTER OF THIS PAGE THAT REPRESENTS YOUR GREATEST ASPIRATION. CREATE A MIND MAP DIAGRAM THAT EXTENDS FROM THAT CENTRAL IDEA.

WHAT IS THE "TAKE AWAY" YOU WANT PEOPLE TO HAVE AFTER MEETING YOU? ON THIS TAKE-OUT CARTON, SKETCH YOUR TAKE AWAY.

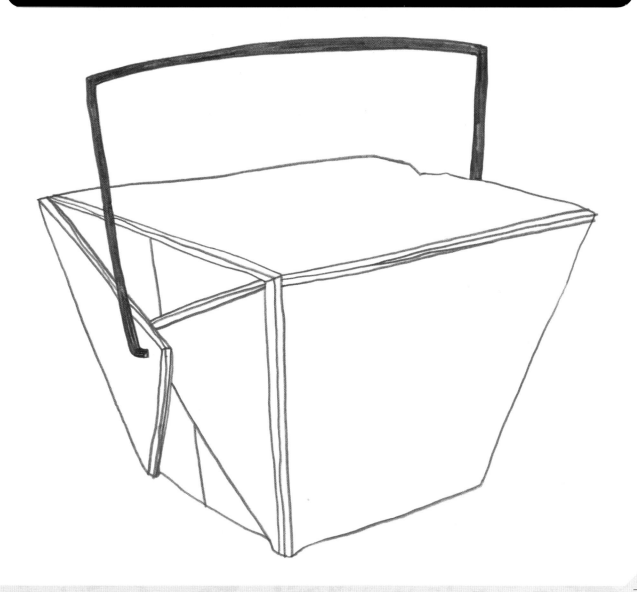

LIST TEN VALUES YOU BELIEVE ARE CRITICAL TO GREAT DESIGN. NOW DELETE SEVEN OF THESE. DROP ANY IDEAS EVERY OTHER DESIGNER WOULD STATE: RESPONSIBLE, HIGH QUALITY, ETC. TAKE THE FINAL THREE THAT ARE MOST PERSONAL. THIS IS YOUR BRAND.

—SEAN ADAMS, ADAMSMORIOKA

LIST THREE OF YOUR EMOTIONAL ATTRIBUTES. SKETCH THEM. LIST THREE OF YOUR FUNCTIONAL OR PRACTICAL STRENGTHS. SKETCH THEM, OR CAST THEM IN A SHORT PLAY.

INVENT THE TITLE OF YOUR MEMOIR—MAKE IT INSTANTLY RECOGNIZABLE. WRITE THE ENDING.

IMAGINE THE TITLE OF AN ARTICLE ABOUT YOUR PROFESSION THAT IS NO MORE THAN 120 CHARACTERS—INCLUDE A KEY TERM PEOPLE USUALLY SEARCH. THEN EDIT IT FOR BREVITY AND BRING IT DOWN TO 70 CHARACTERS.

HOW COULD YOU RUIN YOUR VERBAL IDENTITY? MAKE A LIST OF ALL THE THINGS YOU COULD DO ON TWITTER OR FACEBOOK OR YOUTUBE OR ANY SOCIAL MEDIA PLATFORM THAT WOULD BE INDISCREET.

ASK YOUR BEST FRIEND, YOUR MOM, AND A COLLEGE PROFESSOR TO DESCRIBE YOU IN THREE WORDS. THOSE WORDS SHOULD BE ADDRESSED IN YOUR RÉSUMÉ OR COVER LETTER.

—JAIME LYNN PESCIA

YOU'RE A MAGICIAN. WAVE YOUR MAGIC WAND TO TURN YOURSELF INTO SOMETHING OR SOMEONE ELSE.

YOU'RE A ONE-PERSON BAND. ILLUSTRATE OR WRITE WHAT YOU DO DIFFERENTLY.

INVENT A NEW TOOL BASED ON AN OLD TOOL, OR MERGE TWO TOOLS TO CREATE A NEW ONE.

PROMPTS

TO WHICH FORTUNE 500 COMPANY WOULD YOU COMPARE THE "BRAND OF YOU"? WHY? WRITE YOUR MISSION STATEMENT HERE.

—PAUL RENNER, CREATIVE DIRECTOR

IN EACH MODULE SKETCH OR WRITE SOMETHING KEY ABOUT YOURSELF.

PAIR TWO OPPOSITES. FOR INSTANCE, WRITE ONE SENTENCE ABOUT BEING HIRED. WRITE ONE SENTENCE ABOUT BEING FIRED. WRITE ONE SENTENCE ABOUT THINGS YOU LOVE TO DO. WRITE ONE SENTENCE ABOUT THINGS YOU DISLIKE DOING. WRITE ONE SENTENCE ABOUT GOOD DESIGN AND ONE ABOUT POOR DESIGN, AND SO ON.

> YOU ARE IN AN ELEVATOR WITH A POTENTIAL CLIENT. SELL YOURSELF. WRITE YOUR ELEVATOR PITCH HERE. (FOUR SENTENCES, TOPS!)
>
> —PAUL RENNER, CREATIVE DIRECTOR

IN SEVERAL SENTENCES, EXPLAIN WHAT MAKES YOU DIFFERENT THAN YOUR COMPETITION. THEN, BOIL IT DOWN TO ONE PITHY STATEMENT.

BEGIN A SENTENCE ABOUT YOURSELF WITH "WHAT IF."

LOOK AT A DOOR. WRITE A PARAGRAPH ABOUT WHO PASSES THROUGH THE DOOR. OR, IF THERE WERE A SIGN ON THE DOOR TO ANOTHER WORLD, WHAT WOULD IT SAY AND WHY.

LIST THREE ASSUMPTIONS UPON WHICH YOU BASE YOUR DONNÉE (THE PREMISE ON WHICH YOUR BRAND STORY PROCEEDS). UNDER EACH, LIST THREE THAT STEM OUT.

1.

2.

3.

CONJURING PICTURES: WITH WORDS, TRY TO CREATE A PICTURE IN THE LISTENER'S MIND.

WRITE SOMETHING ABOUT YOURSELF AS IF YOU WERE SOMEONE ELSE—A CELEBRITY, A POLITICIAN, A FILM DIRECTOR.

PROMPTS

WRITE A TRUE STORY ABOUT YOURSELF, FOCUSING ON ONE OR TWO DAYS.

> "DESIGN IS A PLAN FOR ACTION."
> —CHARLES EAMES

CHAPTER THREE

VISUAL IDENTITY

VISUALIZING YOUR BRAND STORY

The form of your personal brand (logo, résumé design, website design, color palette, and any imagery) should communicate your story. We're all familiar with the twentieth-century precept from American architect Louis Sullivan, "Form ever follows function." When it comes to branding, Brian Collins advises, "Form follows fiction."

In the case of personal branding, we could coin it as: Form follows creative nonfiction. Each of us has an evolving creative nonfiction story (the facts of our existence and our practical abilities) combined with a narrative fiction (how we cast ourselves as we evolve personally and professionally). When you tell your story through the design of your personal brand, you give it visual and verbal form. Can your story allow for change as your skills and thinking evolve?

Your brand story will be told across multiple media platforms—print, desktop web, social media, mobile web, and more. Establishing a coherent look and feel across media platforms keeps your solutions unified, so they belong together by resemblance and voice. When someone sees any piece of your visual story, he or she can identify you. Each visual solution is independent, yet should not need to reintroduce itself to viewers.

Each media platform should make a unique contribution to telling your brand story. If the story is told exactly the same way in each medium, then your story is singular rather than dimensional. Each media platform has unique capabilities, which allow you to expand your portrait, your image—exploit those capabilities. Henry Jenkins, who conceived the idea of transmedia storytelling, said:

> "In transmedia, elements of a story are dispersed systematically across multiple media platforms, each making their own unique contribution to the whole. Each medium does what it does best—comics might provide backstory, games might allow you to explore the world, and the television series offers unfolding episodes."
>
> (http://www.fastcompany.com/1745746/seven-myths-about-transmedia-storytelling-debunked)

PAINT THE BROAD PICTURE

Anyone's experience with your personal brand is the product that you're trying to create. Thinking through your goals and attributes, and planning your conception and design development will help you paint your broad picture.

You can establish a minor motif or a complex one. You can take a minor motif and turn it into a major one, too. If you break your story into small parts, you can look for patterns, parallels, and resonances to find thematic similarities. Your design concept does not have to be rigid. For example, a comedic concept can have nuance, with other kinds of emotions or moments, as long as it is unified.

Sean Adams of AdamsMorioka, advises:

> "Being a responsible, skilled and talented designer is the same as a car having reliable wheels. This is the minimum requirement that is expected. What sets great designers apart is the ability to identify the qualities that are unique and personal to their identity, and promoting these relentlessly."

THINK OF BRANDING AS CONNECTING THE DOTS. ALL POINTS OF CONTACT (YOUR COVER LETTER, RÉSUMÉ, BUSINESS CARD, WEBSITE, PROMOTIONAL MATERIALS, ETC.) MUST VISUALLY RELATE AND PROJECT A CONSISTENT MESSAGE. IF ONE PIECE OF COMMUNICATION IS CONSERVATIVE, ANOTHER AGGRESSIVE AND YET ANOTHER DEMURE, YOUR VISUAL VOICE WILL PRESENT AS SPLINTERED, RESULTING IN A CONFUSED CONSUMER WHO DOESN'T KNOW WHAT TO EXPECT WHEN VIEWING A MESSAGE FROM YOU. MOST PEOPLE YOU'RE TALKING TO DON'T KNOW YOU PERSONALLY AND ARE RELYING ON YOUR EFFECTIVE USE OF DESIGN ELEMENTS TO BECOME FAMILIAR AND COMFORTABLE WITH YOUR BRAND.

DEAN JAMES BALLAS, WWW.DEZIGNROGUE.COM

> **"TYPEFACE DESIGN IS A VERY RIGOROUS, ALMOST SCIENTIFIC DISCIPLINE WHERE MINUSCULE VARIATIONS AND ADAPTATIONS REVERBERATE IN MEANING AND IMPACT."**
> —Paola Antonelli, Senior Curator, Department of Architecture and Design, The Museum of Modern Art

Goals

Set some goals for the brand experience. It should:

- Break through via interesting form to capture the prospective employer/client's attention
- Establish an emotional connection
- Induce positive emotions we all want to feel, such as joy, delight or amusement (Psychologist Barbara Fredrickson calls these "wantable" emotions)
- Exhibit your personal best through design and words
- Differentiate yourself using your core values
- Drive the storytelling with intention (make sure to offer a key take away)
- Weave your attributes throughout the "experience"
- Ensure that form follows story

Planning Process

Consider the conception and design process:

- Envision three separate ideas. What is the driver for each concept? Type or image?
- Color palette + typeface(s) + imagery (photography/illustration/graphic interpretations) + patterns/textures
- Create a collage board theme to flesh out the visual thinking.
- Prototype the vision. Revise.

Attributes

Elements	How You Cast Yourself
Authenticity	Élan Vital
Your Promise	Deliverable Benefits
Drivers	Passion and Values
Goals	Relevance
Visual Voice	Visual Interest

Typography

Just like the sound of a specific human voice or musical instrument, every aspect and characteristic of an individual typeface endows those letterforms with a specific visual voice. Typography denotes and connotes—it gives visual denotative form to spoken words as well as communicating on a connotative level. The historical era and provenance of a typeface also implies added meaning to the primary message. Major characteristics that contribute to a typeface's voice are: proportions of the letterforms, shapes of the letterforms, angle of stress, contrast between thick and thin strokes (or no contrast), variation in line width, shape of serifs, etc.

That said, some typefaces have qualities that yield stronger (or radical) voices, giving them a more active, distinctive role in the design solution. Some designers shy away from typefaces whose voices are too loud or quirky. Others use them sparingly.

Other typefaces are more neutral, complementing the image and contextualizing the communication. Some designers think neutral faces can be bland. Others embrace the neutrality. (Designer Massimo Vignelli prefers basic typefaces.) There are typefaces that fall in between those with strong voices and more anonymous faces—those with a soft voice, such as ITC Goudy Sans. Understanding type classifications will help you make informed selections (see Chapter 5).

Type has a visual voice. When you are choosing type, consider these things:

- Select type based on your personal brand concept.
- Type communicates on a denotative (direct meaning) and connotative level (suggested or additional meaning).
- Evaluate type as form based on aesthetic criteria of shape, proportion and balance.
- Evaluate type as shape—it can be rectilinear, curvilinear, geometric or organic.
- Thoughtfully integrate type with imagery.
- Ensure readability.
- Consider context: print or screen and size.
- Spacing can make or break communication.
- Respect margins, which present display and text type.

Type Sense and Sensibility

Do you have design sense as well as sensibility? Design sense means you design with purpose. Sensibility demonstrates your individual ability to respond to the complexities of designing; your discriminating appreciation of the design medium is evident in your work. (Some call it taste.) It is your personal response to design, your mindfulness, your unique capacity to consider every element and take creative leaps. Your sensibility is revealed in typographic details (spacing, typeface selection, typeface pairings, sizing and size relationships); how every graphic element communicates; and how all the graphic elements are considered as players in the story.

CONSIDERATIONS FOR TYPEFACE SELECTION

When you select a typeface for your name or logo, what are you saying about yourself as an individual and as a designer or writer? What are you saying about your taste? Are you bold? Resourceful? Whimsical? Dignified? Energetic? What does the grouping (composition) of the letterforms communicate about you? Are you precise? Mindful? Cheeky? Witty? Suave? Lively?

Select based on your design concept, for readability (how easy or hard it is to read on paper or different screen sizes) and legibility (how easily a person can recognize the letters in a typeface—how the characteristics of each individual letterform are distinguished).

Then consider how aesthetics and function contribute to your brand personality and how the typeface will function.

AESTHETIC CONSIDERATIONS

- How the typeface's visual voice works for your brand personality and visual style
- Serif or sans serif
- Shape of the serif
- Bracketed serifs or serifs without brackets
- What typeface characteristics and qualities communicate on a secondary level
- Aesthetics (impact or beauty) of the letterform proportions
- Type texture—the overall density or tonal quality of a mass of type on a field
- Orientation or lean of axis, or stress
- Overall shape of the letterforms, for example, is the O round or oval?
- Shape of the counters, bowls, and apex
- Do you want low contrast between thick and thin strokes? Extreme thick/thin contrast? Even weight?
- Variation in line width
- Details: serif shape; single-story or two-story construction of a lowercase a and g; tail; bowl; ligatures; finishes
- Select weight based on design concept, content, context and aesthetics
- Variable-width font vs. monospaced

FUNCTIONAL CONSIDERATIONS

- Context: print or screen; close-up or far away
- Size of format: extra small (think business card), small (think mobile viewport), medium (think résumé), large (think desktop web)
- Function: display or text type
- Extensiveness of the font family
- Uppercase, lowercase, unicase
- Included in the font: small caps; italic and oblique; condensed; wide
- Available for screen from a trusted web foundry with print font included
- Web foundry allows for testing font on screen

PAIRING TYPEFACES

One tenet is to design with no more than two typefaces—one for display and one for text.

Most designers pair typefaces for contrast or texture: to complement one another, to differentiate headers from text or to differentiate titles from text. If typefaces are too similar, then the reader might not be able to distinguish them, thus defeating the purpose of using more than one.

Select for contrast, yet choose for similar proportions. Selecting for contrast means mixing typefaces based on differences in structural classifications—for example, mixing a sans serif face with a slab serif face. Do consider how well their proportions work to create harmony. In this category, H&FJ suggests pairing Mercury with Hoefler Tilting (http://www.typography.com). Designer/Illustrator John Sposato suggests pairing Gill Display Compressed (sans) with Bodoni Book (serif), which have a formal resemblance, both based on a similar oval configuration.

Pair complementary typefaces. Select typefaces for contrast but similar x-heights—for example, both ITC Franklin Gothic (strong sans serif) and ITC Century (Modern classification) have tall x-heights. Pair contrasting voices, for example, Didot (Modern classification) and Franklin Gothic Demi (sans serif). Consider pairing typefaces with contrast in weight, for example, Univers family (sans serif) and Serifa family (slab serif, Egyptian).

Pair typefaces with different typographic texture, for example, Helvetica Bold (sans) with American Typewriter Light (serif). Different typographic textures create contrast and visual interest on page or screen.

Choose a type family, extended family or super family or companion typefaces. Utilize any and all from among a family or extended family because all the various weights and styles created for one typeface will still be unified. Super families include both serif and san serif letterforms designed to be used together. Both designed by Emigre, Mr Eaves is the sans-serif companion to Mrs Eaves (serif); Mr Eaves was based on the proportions of Mrs Eaves yet the designer allowed for interesting differences (http://www.emigre.com/EFfeature.php?di=213).

Use decorative faces in small doses. Decorative faces tend to overwhelm a design and designer's personal brand. Consider pairing a decorative typeface (for display only) with a neutral typeface.

> "A LOGO IS THE SMALLEST CANVAS FOR STORYTELLING."
> —GUI BORCHERT, CREATIVE DIRECTOR, 72ANDSUNNY

LOGO: TELLING YOUR VISUAL STORY

A logo tells a visual story. *Your* logo tells *your* story. A logo is a unique identifying symbol. A logo compresses meaning into one small compositional unit, a unit that will be integral to all your visual communication solutions. It can take various forms. Determine which works best to communicate your concept, tell your personal brand story and differentiate you. Here are the form categories:

- **Logotype:** the name is spelled out in unique typography or lettering
- **Lettermark:** the logo is created using your initials or other representative letters
- **Symbol:** a pictorial, abstract, or nonrepresentational visual or letterforms, which may or may not be coupled with your name or studio's name
  - ▶ *Pictorial symbol:* a representational image, resembling or referring to an identifiable person, place, activity or object
  - ▶ *Abstract symbol:* a simple or complex rearrangement, alteration or distortion of the representation of natural appearance, used for stylistic distinction and/or communication purposes
  - ▶ *Nonrepresentational or nonobjective symbol:* purely invented, it does not relate to any object in nature; it does not literally represent a person, place or thing
  - ▶ *Letterform symbol:* letterform(s) used as the symbol, often coupled with one's name
  - ▶ *Character icon:* an avatar, the embodiment of one's personality
- **Combination mark:** a combination of name and symbol
- **Emblem:** a combination of name and images that are inextricably integrated, never separated

> "IF YOU DESIGN A LOGO FOR YOURSELF, IT BETTER BE THE BEST LOGO YOU HAVE EVER CREATED. IF YOU ARE QUESTIONING IF IT IS, THEN IT'S NOT. TRASH IT."
> —JAIME LYNN PESCIA, ART DIRECTOR, DESIGNER, EDUCATOR

Type and Image Relationships in a Logo

To communicate the design concept and your brand personality, type and image should always work cooperatively, in a synergistic manner—the combined effort being greater than the type or image parts alone. Consider three categories of type and image relationships in a logo:

SUPPORTING ROLE

Either type or image(s) has the major role and the other component takes the supporting role and is more neutral.

- A strong visual statement with neutral type in a subordinate role, or…
- Type makes the stronger visual statement and the image takes a supporting role

SHARED CHARACTERISTICS

Type and image share similar defining characteristics. The agreement in form produces consonance.

Congruence relies on agreement in shape, form, treatment/visualization of form, proportion, weight, width, thin/thick strokes, lines, textures, positive and negative shapes, and time period.

CONTRAST

Type and images possess apparent differences, contrasting characteristics. The goal of contrast between type and image characteristics is to produce a unique communication that couldn't exist without the contrast.

Two basic ways type and images work in contrast:

- **Complementary.** Type works in opposition to or in juxtaposition to images, relying on contrasts in shape, form, proportions, weights, widths, thin/thick strokes, lines, textures, positive and negative shapes—for example, geometric versus organic, streamlined versus rough, refined versus sloppy, detailed versus loosely rendered. Mixing styles and historical periods also creates contrast.
- **Ironic.** Typeface and image(s) are incongruous for an ironic effect.

THE LOGO UNIT

As a compositional unit, a logo must be an independent entity, able to stand on its own, not dependent on the corner of a printed page or website screen or dependent upon any particular position within a format. A logo must be a freestanding unit because it is incorporated into many other solutions, such as a résumé, business card and website.

LOCKED UNIT

A logo can be a locked (closed) unit based on basic shapes: circle, square, oval, triangle or trapezoid, as well as other clearly defined shapes. Locked unit logo formats can be organic, rectilinear, curvilinear, irregular and accidental shapes, or recognizable closed shapes (flower, human form, star, tree, animal, etc.). These forms can define the logo's boundaries.

UNLOCKED UNIT

There is a basic unit shape, such as a circle or rectangle, but part of the type or image breaks through the unit, extending into very nearby surrounding graphic space. Yet, unity is maintained.

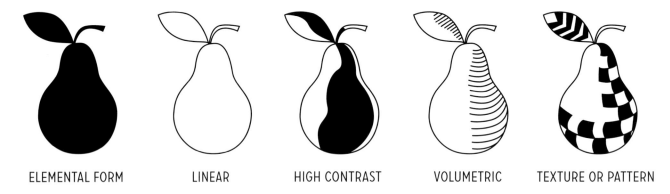

ELEMENTAL FORM | LINEAR | HIGH CONTRAST | VOLUMETRIC | TEXTURE OR PATTERN

Fundamental ways of depicting shapes and the illusion of three-dimensional forms.

FREE-FORM

A logo can be an open free-form shape(s)—not contained or locked by a geometric or other rigid shape acting as the boundary, but still a unit that is independent—a complete stable unit.

VISUALIZATION

How type and image are visualized communicates meaning. Visualizing a dove using a line of varying width will look different and communicate differently than visualizing a dove using extreme light and shadow. The characteristics of all shapes, forms, typefaces, colors, images and symbols of a logo contribute to its denotative and connotative meaning.

Here are fundamental ways of depicting shapes and the illusion of three-dimensional forms.

- **Elemental form:** line or flat tone used to reduce an image or subject to stark simplicity.
- **Linear:** line used as the main element to describe the shape or form. This can be as simple as a notation or as complex as a full-out rendering.
- **High contrast:** depiction of forms based on extreme contrast of light and shadow falling on a three-dimensional form.
- **Volumetric:** light and shadow, gradation or modeling used to suggest the illusion of a three-dimensional form.
- **Texture or pattern:** lines or marks used to suggest form, light, texture, pattern or tone using hatch, crosshatch, cross-contour, dots, smudges and so on.

Line, value and texture also can depict different appearances, such as wood, wire or a carving. Logos can be flat shapes, such as geometric or silhouettes, or imply the illusion of three-dimensional form, such as droplets or spirals.

Logos can have visual textures or imply materials:
- Animal skins
- Brush drawing
- Carving
- Carved ice
- Clay impression
- Cut paper
- Distressed leather
- Fabric
- Hand print
- Metal engraving
- Photographic fragments
- Raised metal
- Torn paper
- Wire
- Wood
- Woodcut

Logos can be flat shapes:
- Curvilinear
- Geometric
- Silhouettes
- Closed
- Open

Logos can be still or animated. They can imply the illusion of three-dimensional forms such as:
- Beveled
- Coil-like
- Cubelike
- Droplets
- Projections outward or canted
- Shadows
- Spirals

CURVILINEAR

GEOMETRIC

SILHOUETTE

CLOSED

OPEN

Types of flat-shaped logos

COLOR

Color communicates on a visceral level. It also can be symbolic or come to represent or be associated with a brand.

People respond to color differently depending on their culture, religion, gender, personal preferences and other variables. The symbolic meaning or cultural association with any color is social and historical, tied to specific experiential contexts. *(See the Glossary of Color in Chapter 5: Resources, for more on symbolism.)*

Color is elusive—it has optical properties that change. Color is physical and also lives in the digital realm. The human brain and eyes perceive color in a relational manner. Any color is seen in relation to other colors that surround it or that are near it. Surrounding colors may alter a color's visual appearance.

To discuss color more precisely, here are three terms to know:

Hue is the name of a color, such as red or violet.

Value refers to the level of luminosity—lightness or darkness of a color.

Saturation (or intensity) is the brightness or dullness of a hue.

ESSENTIAL RELATIONSHIPS ON THE PIGMENT COLOR WHEEL

Whether designing for print or screen, essential color relationships can start with the pigment color wheel, which diagrams basic color harmonies. Three sets of color groups (primary, secondary and interval) comprise the basic pigment color wheel, which designers use as a guide for harmonious color combinations. From there, you can more easily conceive a unique palette—a planned combination of colors—for yourself.

The three primary colors (red, blue and yellow) on the color wheel are connected by an inscribed equilateral triangle, which indicates a basic color group and relationship.

Characteristics: Together as a color palette this basic group of pigment primaries is bold and elemental and may express nostalgia or childlike innocence.

The secondary colors in pigment (orange, green and violet) are mixtures of the primaries. They have less hue contrast among themselves than the primary group because they are mixtures.

Characteristics: Together, as a color palette, they yield a less bold relationship than the primaries, more serene.

Mixtures of the pigment primaries and secondaries yield interval colors between the two: blue (primary) + green (secondary) = blue-green (interval).

WHITE, BLACK AND GRAY

The role of neutrals (white, black and gray, also called achromatic colors) in color relationships varies depending on amounts, positions and the hues they accompany. Within a group of saturated hues, white, black and gray might act as areas of visual rest or chromatic neutrality.

Saturated color as focal point

Depending on amounts, black may darken (as well as deepen) a design, and white may lighten (as well as open up or enlarge) a design. Black-and-white relationships may also be used for contrast, differentiation or drama. Surrounding a saturated hue with grays can turn the high-intensity hue into a focal point.

COLOR TEMPERATURE

A hue may be warm or cool in temperature, which refers to whether the color is associated with warm things (for example, fire or the sun) or cool things (for example, water or grass). The temperature of a color is not absolute but can fluctuate depending on the strength of the dominant hue of a color. For example, a red may contain blue making it look cooler than a warm red-orange. Saturation and value also affect temperature. In print, color temperature is affected by the color of the paper that any ink is printed on. Although it is more difficult to read the temperature of a dark or dull color, these colors do appear warm or cool. Grays mixed from colors, not neutrals, may appear cool or warm as well.

For representational imagery, it is best practice to use a color palette that is either cool or warm. When used in the same design solution, cool and warm colors may visually separate or appear disparate. For example, if you are depicting a green box, it is best to describe all the surfaces with cool values of green, green-grays or a palette of cool tones. If you depict the darker side of the green box with a warm brown or warm gray, the warmer tone will tend to visually separate from the cooler sides and detract from a three-dimensional appearance.

Cool and warm colors in opposition on the color wheel create visual tension or spatial "push-and-pull" effects when composed together.

COLOR: BEST PRACTICE

- Color must be appropriate for your personal brand.
- Color symbolism is not universal—it is culture specific.
- Color is perceived in relation to the hues, values and neutrals that surround it.
- Color can be used to create a focal point.
- Color can differentiate a graphic element from others in a composition.
- Using color is the quickest and easiest way to establish connections among graphic elements in a single composition or across multiple pages.
- Color can be thematic.
- Color can define a section of a website or résumé.

When placed next to one another, a warm color may seem to move forward and a cool color recedes, but this is all relative to the specific composition, amount of color, weight, saturation, value and the position in the composition.

In nonobjective imagery or typography, color temperature can be used for contrast. However, again, be aware that cool and warm colors do tend to appear inconsonant.

COLOR SCHEMES

The color schemes that appear below, harmonious color combinations, are based on hues at full saturation and of middle value range.

When designing with color, always consider hue, value and saturation. Changing the value or saturation of a color will affect how it works and communicates. Also consider how colors will appear and interact on screen or in print. On screen, colors are more luminous. In print, the inert properties of ink applied to paper will look different from when designing them on screen.

Combining the below color schemes with black, white, and gray also affects how they behave and communicate, and can be altered by changes in value and saturation, and by the addition of neutrals.

Monochromatic color schemes employ only one hue. These schemes establish a dominant hue identity while allowing for contrasts in value and saturation.

A monochromatic palette can contribute to a composition's unity and balance. It can appear restrained, simple, and it can act as an alternative to black for a one-color project, which might be a good solution when there are budgetary constraints or if the design concept calls for a monochromatic scheme. (When used on a white screen or paper, a monochromatic scheme based on a hue that is naturally light in value, such as yellow, would not provide enough contrast on its own unless a neutral such as black was added.)

Analogous color schemes employ three adjacent hues. Due to their proximity on the color wheel, analogous colors tend to be a harmonious or congruent color palette. The harmony is created because of the colors' similarity to each another. An analogous color scheme aids establishing unity and calm, like a monochromatic scheme, but it is more diverse. In an analogous scheme, one color can dominate, and the other two colors play supporting roles.

Complementary color schemes are based on a relationship between any two opposing hues on the pigment color wheel. These opposing hues tend to visually vibrate and can express tension or excitement through their strong contrast. Used in small amounts placed close together, complementary colors may mix optically to form grays or to shimmer, which is called *mélange optique* (optical mixture).

Split complementary color schemes include three hues: one color plus the two colors adjacent to its complement on the color wheel. A

Color palettes reach well beyond the pigment color wheel. Color groupings can be found in:

- Nature (earth tones, minerals, the sea, etc.)
- Seasons and climates (autumn, tropical, etc.)
- Fine art (Prehistoric, Fauvism, Pointillism, Divisionism, Mannerism, etc.)
- In global cultures
- Fashion across centuries and countries
- Periods of design history (Psychedelic, New Wave, etc.)
- Textiles (Indian textiles with madder dye; various Native American rugs and weavings, batik, Scot plaids)
- Ceramics (ancient Chinese ceramics, Greek red-figure vase period, etc.)

Always research color symbolism for meaning in relation to the audience, culture, region and country, because each has its own set of associations and meanings.

Beyond color schemes, use color to denote, connote, symbolize, distinguish, differentiate, cue; as themes; to demarcate spatial zones or define a website section, to create emphasis, and more.

split complement's vibratory nature is high contrast but somewhat more diffused than a complement. It is also less dramatic than a complementary color scheme but still visually intense.

Triadic color schemes include three colors that are at equal distance from each other on the color wheel. Basic triadic groups are the primaries and secondaries. An example of another triadic relationship is red-orange/blue-violet/yellow-green. The inherent equalibrium of a triadic group is visually diverse with good hue contrast, yet harmonious.

Tetradic color schemes are comprised of four colors in two sets of complements (a double complementary). Tetradic palettes offer great hue diversity and contrast. For student designers, this palette may be difficult to harmonize unless one hue becomes dominant with the others as supporting players.

Cool colors are the blue, green and violet hues located approximately on the left half of the pigment color wheel. When a composition is based on a cool color palette, it feels synchronized and congruent. Often the resulting effect is calm or serene. Cool colors are easier to balance than warm colors or combined warm/cool palettes.

Warm colors are the red, orange and yellow hues located approximately on the right half of the color wheel. When used together, warm colors look harmonious and are easier to balance than combined warm/cool palettes. The conventional associations with warm colors is the feeling or sensation of heat (fire, the sun), spiciness or intensity.

Résumé, Letterhead and Business Card

A good degree of consistency in look and feel across your résumé, letterhead and business card results in a unified brand, a specific visual appearance and voice. Consider maintaining a color palette or system of color palettes; a typeface or typeface pairings or font family; one logo; a set or system of icons and symbols; and related alignment structures.

Most people start by designing the most complex of these three—the résumé.

However, one could argue that starting with the smallest canvas—the business card—could force you to focus your brand story. (Similarly some designers choose to design for desktop web first because it is the most complex. Others start with mobile first, since it is the smallest canvas and forces critical reductive thinking.)

RÉSUMÉ

Your résumé informs the reader, and identifies and promotes you. Those are three significant functions.

Goals:

- Informs: reader is able to easily glean information
- Identifies: reader recognizes the design as distinct and memorable
- Promotes: fosters the reader's interest in you

There are two fundamental approaches to résumé design. Both avenues will convey your design sense and sensibility.

Inventive (visual or verbal or both) with impeccable typography: Either copy or design or both are inventively expressing a design concept, communicating not only your design skills but your ingenuity in a specific form of wit, whimsy, cool, cheekiness, charm or whatever concept or voice works for your brand.

Straight up and functional with impeccable typography: The design reflects your keen information design skills and typography; the color palette, typefaces(s) and logo or logotype are consistent with your personal brand. This approach stresses clarity of communication, no gimmicks, no overbranding—just unadorned work.

In an article, "Will a Graphic Résumé Get You the Job? The Experts Respond" by Allison Cheston on Forbes.com, when asked about résumé design, Debbie Millman, President, Design, of Sterling Brands, replied, "Substance over style is the rule for *all* résumés.

Any special effects will dilute the gravitas and stature of the impression. You want people to concentrate on your accomplishments and your successes, not the curlicues of a font or unusual shades or contrast of colors." In the same article, Rob Wallace, managing partner and strategic director of Wallace Church, Inc., concurred: "Don't let design disrupt communication."

(http://www.forbes.com/sites/work-in-progress/2012/06/28/will-a-graphic-resume-get-you-the-job-the-experts-respond/)

Concept or Theme?

If you've chosen to design your résumé straight up, then your main considerations have less to do with expressing a design concept (or perhaps even a theme) and more to do with great information design and identifying your brand. It also means maintaining your brand look and feel through color palette, typeface selection, use of rules and other graphic elements, and paper selection. Again, do keep in mind that using this approach does say something about you, your critical thinking and your design sensibility.

If you chose to produce an inventive résumé, then you need to generate a viable design concept or theme that is consistent with your brand personality and voice and express it in effective information design, while promoting your brand.

No matter which approach you choose, flawless typographic design is a must. Your résumé is a sample of your typographic skills. Any potential employer will judge your typographic skills based on your résumé.

Résumé Tips

- Establish an absolutely clear visual hierarchy, because this equals clear communication.
- Be clear. Be pithy.
- Strategic type alignments are key to establishing order.
- Headers should label—but not be more important than the content they title.
- Use rules to divide information. Rules should not call attention to themselves.
- Consider designing and/or utilizing a grid.
- Color identifies, as well as aiding flow through the composition and aiding unity within the composition.
- Select typefaces or a font family that works well with your logo typeface.
- The display and text type do not have to be (or should not be) the same as the typeface of your logo.
- Consider utilizing a font family.
- Consider the text type in a color other than black, unless you deliberately select black (that is, the color of type shouldn't default to black because you didn't consider it).

LETTERHEAD

Printed on a sheet of fine paper or viewed as a digital page, the letterhead is part of your visual identity and acts as a format for formal correspondence. The design of the letterhead should be consistent with other formats in your visual identity, utilizing a similar or related color palette, typefaces and any graphic element or verbal component associated with your personal brand.

Letterhead Design Process

Before you begin the design process, determine how the letterhead will be used (letters, faxes, print and/or digital, invoices). While developing the design, you should explore paper samples to make your paper and envelope selections, as well as determine the production method so that you can guide your visualization process with production and budget parameters in mind. Discussing paper and ink options with a reliable printer helps.

Consider the following points when selecting paper for your letterhead system (business cards, envelopes, proposals, etc.):

- Surface quality and texture (feel and fold the paper)
- Compatibility with laser printers
- Paper color in relation to ink colors and your color palette
- Stock availability
- Content: tree, tree-free or recycled
- Cost
- How the paper takes printing ink (you must see samples)
- How the paper takes pen's ink for a signature
- How the letterhead paper coordinates (in surface quality, texture, and color) with the business card paper (business card paper stock will be heavier)

Which printing process to use:
- Offset lithography
- Gravure
- Flexography
- Screen printing
- Nonimpact (which includes electronically driven ink-jet)
- Letterpress

Specialty processes:
- Embossing
- Engraving (About engraving see *Design To Touch* by Rose Gonnella)
- Watermark
- Foil stamping

Fundamentals of Letterhead Design

Every design decision counts, from the typography to the placement of the contact information. Whether you specify the paper's weight or choose the color palette, each aspect of the design is an opportunity to present a consistent identity. Function and coherent identity elements are imperatives.

Function: Leave sufficient room for correspondence.

Size: The U.S. standard size is 8.5" × 11", which is also used in Mexico and Canada. Other countries use the metric system of measurement for letterhead and envelopes.

Digital: Your budget for print might limit your color selection, but you can use as many colors as you like for a PDF (unless you expect someone to print it out).

Fax: The letterhead should be legible when faxed.

Folds: A letterhead is folded to fit into a standard-size envelope. The composition should take the folds into account. Also, the paper selection should hold up to folding and should not crack or bulge.

Ink: The letterhead paper and envelope should take printing ink, laser printer ink and pen ink well.

Composition

Very often the pertinent information resides at the head (or top) of the page—hence the term letterhead. That kind of arrangement leaves ample room for correspondence. Some designers split the information and position some at the foot, or bottom, of the page. Others break with tradition and position type, graphics or illustrations in any number of ways—in a vertical direction at the left or right side, all over the page in light or ghosted values or colors, or around the perimeter of the page.

Information should be in a logical information hierarchy; for example, the zip code should not be the first thing the reader notices.

Your name or logo is usually the most prominent element on the letterhead.

All other type and images should be arranged accordingly, from the most important to the least important.

A graphic element other than your name or logo can be the most prominent element in a design as long as it is relevant.

Having slight to moderate variations in color, type or arrangements among the résumé, letter-head, envelopes and business cards can work, depending on how you manage the variation. A unified stationery system can incorporate great variety.

Business Card

A business card quickly and directly tells its reader who you are, what you do, with whom you are affiliated and how to contact you. A business card is a printed or digital surface—a small rectangle, most often—on which your name, business affiliation and contact information are printed. Since business cards must include critical contact information and your logo on a small surface, usually no other information is included. Limiting the amount of information on a business card can aid a viewer's ability to glean information.

To include more information or graphics, some design a two-sided card, utilizing the reverse side. Although most cards do not have printed information on the reverse side, some designers find it a wonderful canvas for expanding their brand story.

Standard content includes:
- Your name
- Job title(s)
- Studio or other entity
- Address or office location
- Phone and fax numbers
- Email address(es)
- Web address

Signs, Symbols and Icons

Symbols and icons have become more important to a personal identity because they play significant roles in screen media, on websites, mobile apps, social media and more. When icons function as part of a larger personal branding program, their design is considered in relation to the broader context and program, ensuring they function as stand-alone solutions that achieve communication goals, as well as within the broader personal brand program.

Designing a system requires a workable design concept and a consistent use of scale, perspective, shapes and formal elements, such as line, color and texture. The signs or icons in a system must look as if they belong to the same family. Establish a firm design concept, style and vocabulary of shapes so the system looks like it was created by one hand and mind for your brand language.

Use of Signs and Symbols

Some symbols take on greater meaning than others due to their context and roles in religion, culture, history or society. Examples include the yin–yang (the Chinese symbol of the interplay of forces in the universe), the cross in Christianity, and the Kokopelli associated with the American Southwest and its Native American cultures. A circle with a few lines in it designed by Gerald Holtom in 1956 to symbolize nuclear disarmament came to stand for the idea of peace.

Signs and symbols are reductive images, serving many functions in visual communication, with many crossing language and cultural barriers. A classification of signs helps us understand how to use them:

Sign: a visual mark or a part of language that denotes another thing. For example, the word cat and a pictograph of a cat are both signs used to represent "cat"; the % denotes percentage; the written letter A is a sign for a spoken sound.

Icon: an image (pictorial image or symbol) used to represent objects, actions and concepts. Often an icon resembles the thing it represents. It can be a photograph, a pictorial representation or an elemental image, such as the trashcan screen icon or the wheelchair accessibility icon.

Index: a sign that signifies a direct relationship between the sign and the object, without resembling the thing signified. There are a variety of ways this happens: as a cue that makes the viewer think of the reference (for example, smoke is an indexical sign for fire), by its proximity to it (for example, a diver down flag means someone is under water and you must steer clear of the area), by actually pointing to the thing signified (an arrow at an intersection on a roadside) or by being physical evidence of it (for example, a hoof print on the ground).

Symbol: a visual that has an arbitrary or conventional relationship between the signifier and the thing signified. We understand the meaning of symbols through learned associations (for example, an olive branch is a symbol of peace; a heart shape means love; a pink-colored ribbon signifies breast cancer awareness).

Icons

Across media, you have many of the same considerations:

- Who is the audience? Prospective employers? Clients? Award-show judges?
- At what size will the icons be seen?
- What is the context and where will the icons be seen—on screen, close-up, lighted, from a distance, in print? At which perspective or angle? 2-D or 3-D?
- What are your communication goals? What do the icons represent: actions, figures, places, objects, creatures, your skills?
- How reductive or elemental do they need to be to work?
- Are the icons part of a system? Part of your personal brand iconography or language? Does the form follow your story?
- Which style will work across the system and is appropriate for your identity?

ICON DESIGN TIPS

Accurately depict the shape of the object to allow people to recognize and understand the icon at a glance.

Aim for elemental form. Economy of form trumps intricacy or complexity. Details and any excess information may not read well, especially on smaller screens.

Represent an image from its most characteristic angle.

Select commonly recognizable images that people across cultures will be able to understand.

Select color and/or tones for impact, legibility, meaning, personal brand storytelling and context (for example, icons inside toolbar buttons versus icons on a mobile home screen).

Treat all icons in a system consistently in terms of style of visualization, perspective, and near and far. For example, as a general rule, if one icon is cropped, they should all be cropped. If one icon is seen in full view straight on, all should be depicted similarly.

Use a consistent single light source on all icon objects, if using light and shadow to depict form.

Visualize icons to work well on both white and black backgrounds.

Scale the icon for different sizes (1,024 × 1,024 pixels; 512 × 512 pixels; 256 × 256 pixels; 128 × 128 pixels; 32 × 32 pixels; 16 × 16 pixels).

SYMBOLS & AVATARS

The avatars you create for yourself are symbolic. Any image you conceive, illustrate and design to represent you or your brand is a symbol of you, your skills, sensibility and personality. You can have one, or you can have a symbol system. You can utilize flowers, fauna, trees, forms derived from nature, mythological creatures, objects or any image to represent you if those images work conceptually; for example, see Seunghyun Shon's logo, a tree, in Chapter 4. *(For a Glossary of Symbols, see Chapter 5: Resources.)*

Symbols and avatars help define you in social media and sharing sites. You can even incorporate symbols other illustrators or designers create for you, with their permission, and if the avatars or symbols work for your personal brand. Other than copyright-free images (whether in the public domain or offered by stock houses as promotions), most photographs, illustrations and graphic representations found on the Internet or in print publications are intellectual property (original creative work that is legally protected) belonging to other visual artists. If you use found images, you must obtain permission from the copyright holder. If you use stock images from an archive or a stock house, you must purchase them and understand the licensing agreement and how the rights are managed.

Tips for Digital Media

- Treat your website as rich media; exploit its capabilities.
- Use Google Maps, if relevant to your concept.
- Use Google Resources.
- Develop a digital presence. (Flavors.me automatically organizes your web presence. Visit http://flavors.me.)
- Determine whether scrolling or clicking best suits your content and concept.

WEBSITE

A streamlined visual layout provides an immediate sense of location at all times, one that offers consistent elements from page to page.

A plan is necessary for leading the viewer through the site. Again, to sustain your personal brand, there should be some consistency among media platforms—however, a website has unique capabilities (sound, motion, links) to tell your brand story. Use it as rich media, if relevant.

The home page is the primary entrance to a website. Along with a central navigation system, it gives the visitor contact information and establishes the visual look and feel of your site. The home page can set the tone for the entire website experience.

The colors, graphics, textures and spatial illusions set up an emotional level of expressiveness.

If the home page displays moving graphics that twist, turn and flip, the visitor will expect playful activity throughout the site. A home page with minimal still imagery and lots of negative graphic space will cause visitors to expect this same minimalism everywhere else on the site.

When judging websites for merit, there are basic criteria such as:
- content
- structure and navigation
- visual design
- functionality
- interactivity
- overall experience

A design concept is the driving idea—the backbone—of the planning for any interactive solution based on the content, strategy and goals. Formulating a theme is similar to design concept development. If you can identify a theme that best tells your brand story, that theme can be a consistent design element throughout to drive the flow of the design. Visual design is a marriage of form and function and story to ensure an effortless and worthwhile user experience.

A grid is most often used as the central ordering structure for a website. It is a framework used to create a uniform layout from page to page, while allowing for some variation. Design the digital space for ease of use and flow from one page—or space or graphic component—to another. Thoughtfully delineate the parameters for content areas: Use as many subdivisions as needed and negative spaces based on content, communication goals and screen(s) and platform. Then test the grid to see if it can accommodate the content.

The grid design should accommodate the project's needs, reaping the benefit of its structure without having to break the grid often or at all. We often think of a web page as a fixed page design rather than one screen in a fluid online experience. How each web page is constructed and how each page moves (or scrolls) to the next is critical.

Keep in mind:
- Your website is part of your identity, but it also showcases your work, as if it were an online museum or guided tour.
- The website design shouldn't overwhelm the work.
- Information and images are presented in chunks, which make it easier for the viewer to read and stay focused. Aspects of the information chunks can change while most else stays the same. Modular grids work well to present many images.
- The chunks must be unified by an underlying structure and an overall design.

BYOB CHECKLIST

My brand personality is: _____

    This is strategic because: _____

My communication goals are: _____

Ask: Are these all the things I want people to think about me or not?

My brand voice is: _____ [relaxed], [formal], [whimsical], [free spirited], [serious], [bold], [authentic]

Expressed through this visualization technique my style says: _____
_____

Color palette is: _____

    My color palette communicates: _____

Logo typeface(s): _____

    This typeface communicates the following about me: _____
_____

Typeface pairings or font family for résumé, business card, website: _____

    This typeface pairing or font family works for my brand because: _____
_____

This typeface pairing or font family is readable and legible in print and on screen because:

My brand is: Unique [ ]   Recognizable [ ]   Memorable [ ]   Definitely me [ ]

Additional thoughts: _____
_____
_____
_____
_____

INTERVIEW WITH MATTEO BOLOGNA
MUCCA DESIGN

BIO: Matteo Bologna is the founding partner and principal of Mucca Design, where he also serves as creative director.

Under his direction, the Mucca Design team has solved numerous design challenges and created uniquely successful work for a wide variety of companies like Victoria's Secret, André Balazs Properties, Barnes & Noble, Rizzoli, Starr Restaurants, Patina Restaurant Group, Adobe Systems, and Target.

The work produced by the Mucca Design team has been widely recognized by industry publications, competitions and exhibitions, including the AIGA, *Communication Arts*, *Eye*, *Graphis*, *HOW*, *Print*, the Type Directors Club, the Art Directors Club and the James Beard Foundation.

Matteo is the vice president of the Type Directors Club. He frequently lectures about branding and typography around the world.

Q: *Is there a way to know which typefaces will work together? Can you offer three tips for pairing typefaces?*

Typefaces are telling us stories. The rules we need to use are based on the effect that you want to suggest as a designer. For instance, if you want to tell a story that has Victorian taste, then, well, you have to sparkle your page with several different typefaces.

But if you do so, you have to wear the identity of a printer from the period and use digital type like it was lead type picked from a type case. If you need a headline, you should try not to scale in size a typeface that was designed as a body text font, instead you will pick a display face. For this reason you will need to know about the history of every typeface you are using to make your storytelling believable.

Q: *You've said, "Type has the power to suggest and add nuances to the message." Would you explain this further, please? How does this relate to designing one's personal brand identity?*

We are all influenced by what we see most. A curly font will mean "feminine" or "childish." A Spencerian script will tell you "formal" or "celebratory." Every object on a page has a meaning, but the shape of the letters is giving extra meanings to the words they are composing.

Q: *What advice can you offer about designing with type for a résumé? Personal website?*

Clarity is the main goal of a résumé. But also personality. So the job of the designer is to be the alchemist who is able to manage these ingredients to produce a promotional piece that talks about you and about your capability as a designer at the same moment.

PROMPTS

> FROM THE TEN TYPEFACES ON THIS PAGE, SELECT TWO THAT DO NOT REPRESENT YOUR PERSONALITY. CIRCLE THE PARTS OF THE TYPEFACES THAT INFLUENCED YOUR DECISION. THEN RELATE AN ADJECTIVE TO EACH CHARACTERISTIC THAT INFLUENCED YOUR CHOICES.

Franklin Gothic

Didot

Rockwell

Serifa

ITC Century

Centaur

Univers 45 or 55

Gills Sans

Optima

Bauer Bodoni

FROM THE TEN TYPEFACES ON THIS PAGE, SELECT AT LEAST TWO THAT TYPIFY YOUR PERSONALITY. CIRCLE THE PARTS OF THE TYPEFACES THAT INFLUENCED YOUR DECISION. THEN RELATE AN ADJECTIVE TO EACH CHARACTERISTIC THAT INFLUENCED YOUR CHOICES.

News Gothic

Didot

Adobe Garamond

Serifa

Rockwell

Centaur

Futura

Gills Sans Extra Bold Condensed

City Bold

Roman Compressed

CONSIDER DIFFERENT EMOTIVE STATES, LIKE "PLAYFUL," "DARING," "CONFIDENT," AND "BRASH." TYPESET THOSE WORDS IN FONTS THAT MATCH THE EMOTIONAL SPACE. THEN MIX IT UP. WHAT DO YOU FIND?

—MELANIE WIESENTHAL, CREATIVE DIRECTOR

LOGO UNITS: WITHIN EACH SHAPE, SKETCH THE SAME OBJECT, SUCH AS A TREE, KEY, OR CRAB, TO REALIZE HOW EACH FORM RELATES TO THE SHAPE OF THE FORMAT.

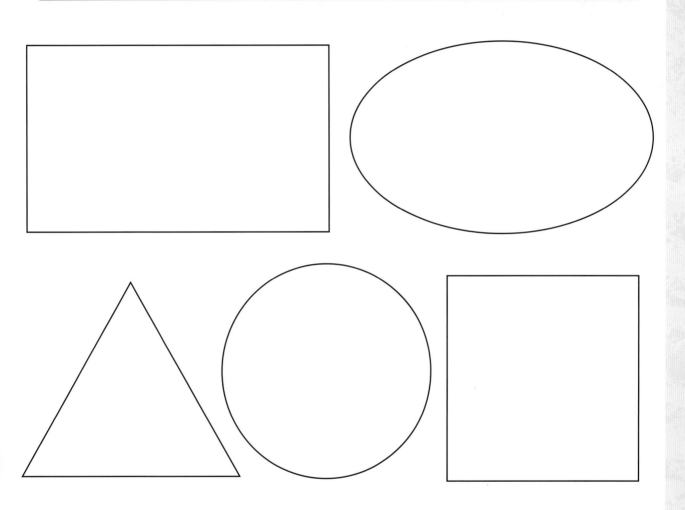

DESIGN A SYMBOL THAT ENCOMPASSES THE ESSENCE OF YOUR NAME.

—JAIME LYNN PESCIA, ART DIRECTOR, DESIGNER, EDUCATOR

WHICH COUNTER SHAPE ARE YOU? WHICH LOWERCASE "G"? WHICH UPPERCASE "M"? WHY? WHICH SERIF ARE YOU? FIND AN ADJECTIVE TO DESCRIBE EACH.

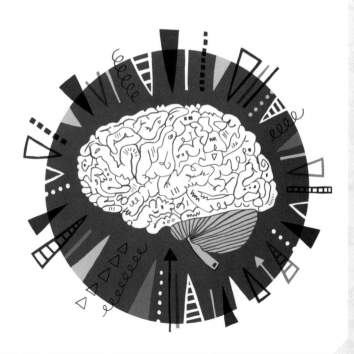

TO SELECT A TYPEFACE, START CONCEPTION BY CHOOSING A SPECIFIC SERIF. THEN MOVE ON TO SELECTING COUNTER SHAPES YOU LIKE. CAN YOU EXTRAPOLATE ON AN ELEMENT FROM THE SERIF OR COUNTER SHAPE?

START BY SELECTING A TYPEFACE FOR THICK/THIN CONTRAST. DO THOSE WIDTH RELATIONSHIPS WORK FOR YOUR BRAND STORY? OR WOULD AN EVEN WEIGHT STROKE LETTERFORM WORK BEST?

THE BASIC OUTER SHAPE OF A LOGO CAN BE A CIRCLE, RECTANGLE, TRIANGLE OR FREE-FORM. INSCRIBE YOUR NAME IN EACH SHAPE ON THIS PAGE.

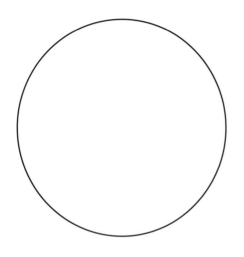
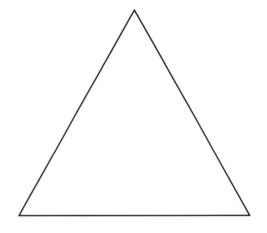

THINK ABOUT WHICH ONE (OR TWO) OF YOUR FIVE SENSES IS MOST ACUTE. CREATE A LOGO THAT REFLECTS THAT SENSE.

—NANCY NOVICK, WRITER AND BLOGGER AT WWW.STACKED-NYC.COM

LIFEBOAT: IMAGINE THAT YOU ARE GETTING INTO A LIFEBOAT AND CAN ONLY TAKE A FEW THINGS WITH YOU. PICK ONE WORD, ONE COLOR, ONE FONT, ONE IMAGE, ONE NAME, ONE SONG, ONE FOOD, ONE SCENT.

—STEPHEN T. HALL, PROFESSOR OF ADVERTISING, SAVANNAH COLLEGE OF ART AND DESIGN

LANDMARKS: DEVELOP ICONS ABOUT YOURSELF TO FIT IN A MAP. INCLUDE FOUR INTERESTING ASPECTS ABOUT YOURSELF THAT ARE EASY TO SHARE WITH OTHERS. DEVELOP IMAGES THAT REPRESENT EACH ASPECT. WHAT WOULD BE THE GENERAL THEME BY WHICH YOU WILL CALL THIS GEOGRAPHY?

—JULIA NEVÁREZ, PH.D. ENVIRONMENTAL PSYCHOLOGY, KEAN UNIVERSITY

SKETCH FIVE DIFFERENT SHAPES THAT COULD REPRESENT YOU. MAKE TWO LOCKED UNITS. CREATE ONE UNLOCKED UNIT. SKETCH TWO OPEN, FREE-FORM UNITS.

WRITE YOUR NAME SEVERAL TIMES USING AN UNUSUAL WRITING OR DRAWING IMPLEMENT. FOR EXAMPLE, WRITE WITH A ROSEBUD DIPPED IN BLACK COFFEE.

SELECT TWO COLORS TO REPRESENT EACH OF THE FOLLOWING: SERENE, WHIMSICAL, EDGY, SUAVE, IRREVERENT.

MOOD BOARD: MAKE A COLLAGE OF PICTURES AND WORDS THAT REPRESENT PERSONAL THINGS YOU HAVE CHOSEN FOR YOURSELF, FOR EXAMPLE, YOUR FAVORITE ARTICLE OF CLOTHING, OR YOUR SIGNATURE FOOD, OR THE NAME OF YOUR PET.

—STEPHEN T. HALL, PROFESSOR OF ADVERTISING, SAVANNAH COLLEGE OF ART AND DESIGN

SKETCH OR WRITE ABOUT ONE ANIMAL OR TREE THAT REPRESENTS YOUR INTELLECT.

SKETCH OR WRITE ABOUT ONE ANIMAL OR TREE THAT REPRESENTS YOUR PERSONALITY.

THINK OF AN EXISTING BRAND. CONSTRUCT A MEANINGFUL STORY AROUND THE BRAND BASED ON RESEARCH. THEN REDESIGN ITS IDENTITY BASED ON WHAT YOU NOW KNOW.

—MELANIE WIESENTHAL, CREATIVE DIRECTOR

ONCE YOU HAVE DRAFTED YOUR LOGO, SHARE IT WITH TEN PEOPLE INDIVIDUALLY. ASK THEM:

- WHAT DO YOU SEE?
- WHAT DO YOU THINK?
- WHAT DO YOU FEEL?

ARE YOU EXCITED BY THEIR RESPONSES?

—ZANDRA GRATZ, PH.D., PSYCHOLOGY, KEAN UNIVERSITY

DESIGN A REPRESENTATIONAL SYMBOL FOR YOURSELF.

DESIGN AN ABSTRACT SYMBOL FOR YOURSELF.

INVENT A NONOBJECTIVE SYMBOL FOR YOURSELF.

YOU'VE MADE IT TO WHERE YOU WANT TO BE IN FIVE YEARS. SKETCH THE ICON THAT APPEARS ON YOUR OFFICE DOOR.

CONCEIVE AND SKETCH AN IMAGE THAT WOULD PRIMARILY REPRESENT YOU. MAKE IT A LOGO OR A PRIMARY AVATAR.

> LIST TEN VALUES YOU BELIEVE ARE CRITICAL TO GREAT DESIGN. NOW DELETE SEVEN OF THESE. DROP ANY IDEAS EVERY OTHER DESIGNER WOULD LIST: RESPONSIBLE, HIGH QUALITY, ETC. TAKE THE FINAL THREE THAT ARE MOST PERSONAL. THIS IS YOUR BRAND.
>
> —SEAN ADAMS, ADAMSMORIOKA, INC.

1.
2.
3.
4.
5.
6.
7.
8.
9.
10.

DRAW YOUR FACEBOOK® STATUS. DRAW ANOTHER ONE.

SKETCH YOUR TWITTER PAGE BACKGROUND USING ICONS OR SYMBOLS YOU CREATED FOR YOUR BRAND. OR USE ELEMENTS OF YOUR SELECTED TYPEFACE TO DO THE SAME.

CHAPTER FOUR
CASE STUDIES

Debbie Millman
President, Design/Sterling Brands

Debbie Millman is president of the design division at Sterling Brands. She has been there for 17 years and in that time she has worked on the redesign of over 200 global brands, including projects with Pepsi, P&G, Colgate, Nestlé and Hasbro.

Debbie is president emeritus of the AIGA, the largest professional association for design in the world. She is a contributing editor at *Print* magazine and co-founder and chair of the Masters in Branding Program at the School of Visual Arts in New York City. In 2005, she began hosting the first weekly radio talk show about design on the Internet. The show is titled "Design Matters with Debbie Millman" and it is now featured on DesignObserver.com. In 2011, the show was awarded a Cooper Hewitt National Design Award.

She is the author of five books on design and branding including, *How to Think Like a Great Graphic Designer* (Allworth Press, 2007), *Look Both Ways: Illustrated Essays on the Intersection of Life and Design* (HOW Books, 2009) and *Brand Thinking and Other Noble Pursuits* (Allworth, 2011).

www.sterlingbrands.com
www.debbiemillman.com

Millman logo sketches by Doyald Young. The final logo appears at the right.

Debbie Millman

you can be anywhere when your life begins

Millman banner and website screenshots. Millman pixel illustration by Christoph Niemann.

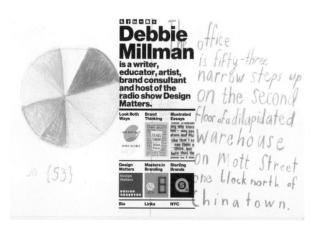

Millman's Facebook page (above) and Twitter page (below).

The cover of Millman's book Brand Thinking (left) and an image for the "Design Matters with Debbie Millman" internet radio show (above).

PAUL RENNER
Creative Director

Paul Renner started his ad career as an art director, which led to senior art director, which led to associate creative director, which led to creative director, which became global creative director… and he is now freelancing, which means he can be any of the previously mentioned at any given time. Paul Renner has lived in New Jersey, working at W+K, Philly; then San Francisco at Goodby, Silverstein & Partners and Butler, Shine, Stern & Partners; then Boston at Arnold Worldwide; then New York City at W+K; and then New Jersey again at Anomaly. Paul Renner started his ad career drinking Budweiser while working on accounts like Subaru, Sega, Pizza Hut, Volkswagen, ESPN, Jordan, Carnival Cruise Lines, BMW and most recently… Budweiser. Paul Renner believes in full circles.

Building My Own Brand

The RENNER logo plays off the fact that the word "renner" is a palindrome; you can read it frontwards and backwards. I wanted something bold and graphic that highlighted that without being too heavy handed or cartoony.

The site includes almost all the work I touched over twenty-two years in the business. I wanted people to get lost in there and hopefully connect with something. If someone goes on my site and can't find anything they like, I've failed!

RENNER

THE WORK   THE INFO

BECAUSE OF ADVERTISING, I HELD A BABY CHIMP, PARTIED WITH U2, SHOOK DR J'S HAND, CREATED A PEN NAME, CAUGHT JACQUELINE SMITH CHECKING ME OUT, LAUNCHED A NEW ESPN NETWORK, SAW A WOMAN MAKE NUMBER TWO ON A NYC STREET, HUGGED FERGIE, MADE A CLIENT CRY, WAS SURROUNDED BY SPORT LEGENDS, HAD GENE SIMMON'S CELL PHONE NUMBER, WORKED WITH SOME OF THE MOST TALENTED CREATIVE MINDS IN THE WORLD, SAT ONE ROW BEHIND JACK AT A LOS ANGELES LAKERS GAME...WE CAN CHAT ABOUT MANY MORE OVER A BEER SOMETIME...

I FINALLY HAVE ALL MY WORK IN ONE PLACE. THE DIGITAL WORLD THAT WE LIVE IN, MAKES THAT VERY EASY TO DO. MAYBE TOO EASY. PROBABLY SHOULD HAVE EDITED MORE. BUT, SCREW IT. LOOK AROUND. I HOPE YOU FIND SOMETHING YOU CAN LAUGH, CRY, OR MAYBE, IF I AM LUCKY, CONNECT TO.

RENNER

PAUL RENNER ART DIRECTOR / CREATIVE DIRECTOR 609.558.9022

paul_renner@me.com

THE WORK

2011-present
anomaly
Global Creative Director, Budweiser

2010
RENNER.ink
Freelance art / creative director

2007-2010
ARNOLD Boston
Creative Director on Carnival Cruise Lines
Sniper on ESPN, Progressive Insurance, Foot Joy

2003-2007
W+K NYC
Creative Director on ESPN

1998-2003
ARNOLD Boston
Associate Creative Director on Volkswagen of America

1996-1998
HOUSTON, HERSTEK, FAVAT Boston
Senior Art Director on Converse, Mass. Department of Health

1995-1996
BUTLER, SHINE & STERN
Art Director on Sci-fi Channel, Northgate Mall, Howell Central Little League, Anheuser-Busch\

1993-1995
GOODBY, SILVERSTEIN & PARTNERS SF
Art director on Sega and Pizza Hut

1991-1993
W+K PHILADELPHIA
Art Director on Subaru, ESPN, Philadelphia Inquirer

Rich Arnold

Senior Visual Designer, Huge, Inc.

Rich Arnold lives and works in Brooklyn, New York. He's currently a senior visual designer with Huge, Inc., and looking forward to the next opportunity to discuss the merits of Bruce Springsteen.

Building My Own Brand

With my identity, I've tried to be as personable as possible. My Twitter and Facebook [feeds] both consist mostly of jokes and anecdotes, and I don't shy away from vulgarities on either. I do my best to make sure that my identity is as much of an honest reflection of myself as I can.

Visually, I try to keep things as clean and muted as possible. Two faces, two colors and as much white space as can be afforded. The star here is the work, so all I'm attempting to do is to put it in a frame that complements it. If I go to a designer's portfolio and I come away with a memory of the site and not the work, then that's a failure.

RICH ARNOLD
908.591.9007
deadeyedesignny.com
richarnold@ deadeyedesignny.com

OBJECTIVE
Make great design, be pixel perfect, avoid poverty, and above all else, enjoy every bourbon.

EXPERIENCE
HUGE INC.
Ad Age #9 Agency A-List, 2012
Senior Visual Designer
2011 – Present

ST. MARTIN'S PRESS
Pulitzer Prize winning publisher
Designer
2008 – 2011

MARVEL COMICS
Spider-Man's Dad
Intern
2007

EDUCATION
BFA Visual Communications
Graphic Design
2008 Kean University

INFLUENCES

Vonnegut   Rand   Bass   Calrissian

ACKNOWLEDGMENTS
- Selected to the ADCNY National Student Portfolio Review
- Selected to the One Club Annual Exhibition

SKILLS
Photoshop
Illustrator
Indesign
After Effects
Dreamweaver

SPENDS TOO MUCH MONEY ON
Records
Concerts
Comic Books
Coffee

RICH ARNOLD

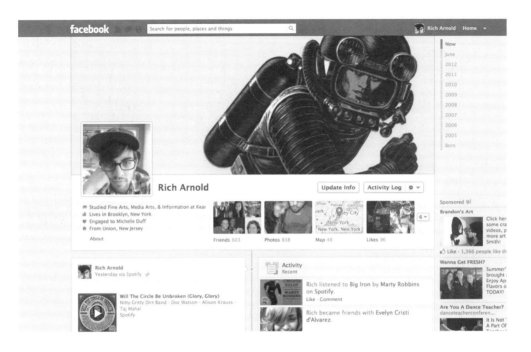

Arnold's Facebook page (far top left), Twitter page (far bottom left), portfolio landing page (left) and logo (above)

SEUNGHYUN SHON
Graphic Designer

Seunghyun Shon is a graphic designer and web designer with experience in Korea and the USA. Some of her clients include Samsung, Kefico, Fox Korea and Disney Korea. Also, Seunghyun has worked in University Relations at Kean University.

Born in Seoul, Korea, Seunghyun enrolled in graduate studies in the USA and received a masters degree in graphic communication management from the Robert Busch School of Design at Kean University in New Jersey.

Building My Own Brand

Trees change in color and mode with the seasons.
I wish to design a variety of projects.

Each part of a tree—such as the root, branch and leaf—is useful.
I wish to be a useful and helpful person.

When my mom was having me, she had a dream about a luxuriant tree.

Trees make me feel calm and refreshed.

Seunghyun Shon

SEUNGHYUN SHON

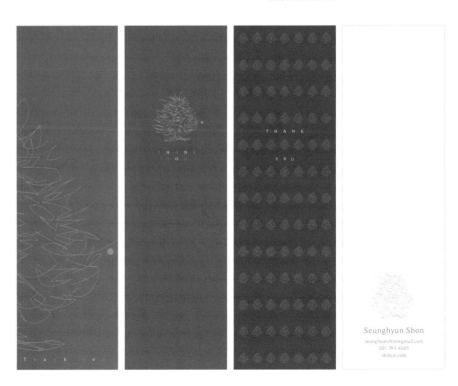

SEUNGHYUN SHON

Seunghyun Shon

seunghyunshon@gmail.com
201. 783. 4005
shshon.com

Manik Rathee
User Experience Engineer at Obama for America

Most recently, Manik Rathee was a designer, user experience engineer & front-end developer working for Barack Obama's reelection campaign: Obama For America.

Manik graduated from Kean University with a BFA degree in graphic design & advertising. He has worked as a freelance designer for various companies including AT&T and Sprint, as well as subsidiaries of Apple, Inc. In 2010, Manik joined RevSystems, Inc., an interactive design firm based out of central New Jersey, as their lead designer. He worked on various projects ranging from branding to iPhone applications to websites—including several responsive websites, which were the first of their kind. He led the design team at RevSystems until November 2011, when he was offered the position with the Obama Campaign. His final project at RevSystems was rethinking the entire agency brand and launching a completely redesigned responsive website. The redesign has been featured on many design blogs because of its use of modern web technologies in conjunction with stunning typography. In January of 2012, he moved to Chicago and began working on the President's campaign as a user experience engineer and front-end developer. He has worked on various entities under the campaign, such as the "Barack Obama Dashboard" and the "Call Tool." Most notable, however, was his involvement in the redesign of www.BarackObama.com, which became the first responsive political website in history.

Building My Own Brand

My visual identity consists of a simple black-and-white square, with a cropped lowercase "m." The symbol represents the minimalistic style of my design work: organized hierarchy and simple shapes.

The symbol is carried through all of my work, from my personal landing page to my online portfolio, and all the way through my social profiles (Twitter, Facebook, etc.).

The consistency of the brand image across all media means that people can instantly recognize one of my online entities.

manik rathee
230 lorraine ave, apt 3
montclair, nj 07043

732.208.0480
manik@manikrathee.com

manikrathee.com

technical proficiency:
platforms: windows, osx, ios
version control/git, jekyll
adobe creative suite 3-5, adobe lightroom, byrce 3d studio, final cut pro
html5, css3, jquery

artistic proficiency:
web design, responsive & valid techniques.
branding & identity
advertising & copywriting, print & web
web/mobile/ios applications, ui design for jquim framework
video filming & editing
photography (dslr) and photo retouching

education:
rutgers university - 2006 – 2008
as psychology
honors college
head photographer, ru observer
  - student newspaper

kean university - 2008 – 2011
*bfa visual communications
/ advertising*
deans list: fall 2008-spring 2011

experience:
user experience engineer - barack obama / january 2012 - present
www.barackobama.com
managed user experience for obama for america web products including the Call Tool and www.barackobama.com. worked with optimisation and user testing to provide the most advanced and user-friendly donation platform in the history of modern politics to millions of visitors. also developed the world's first "quick donate" actions and mobile buttons.

graphic, ui design lead - revsystems, inc / november 2010 - january 2012
www.revsystems.com
led a team of five designers in creating designs for web & applications. web designs included custom wordpress themes, mobile and responsive websites, corporate websites, as well as e-commerce designs. applications include custom web apps, jquery ui Mobile skinning and iphone os design for iphone and ipad. all projects included wireframing and ux flow mapping.

web designer - hartz mountain corp / march 2010 - october 2010
www.hartz.com
worked on an expansive network of websites stemming from hartz.com. handled page creation on development servers to packaging/deployment to staging and live servers. designed user interfaces for touts and interactive panels of the website. also filmed & edited product demos for b2b distribution.

twitter   @manikrathee
dribbble /manikrathee
github   /manikrathee

MANIK RATHEE

DESIGN & DEVELOPMENT

Blog.manikrathee.com is my newly designed blog. The entire layout is a custom responsive wordpress build that I created as a "one hour project." I spent under an hour doing all of the layout, design, developement and testing. It is still in its infancy with less than ten posts but I plan to expand it with technical posts regarding responsive design and new css3/html5 techniques.

QUICK VIEW

CLIENT
Personal Blog

PROJECT TYPE
Responsive Blog & CMS

TARGET DEVICES
Desktop / Mobile

VIEW PROJECT

PROCESS

I have been taking on multiple short side projects from day to day, ranging from tumblr themes to wordpress sites. This blog, as stated above, was created in under one hour. It is built using the 1140gs, so it is responsive, html5 boiler, fit-text and multiple other jquery items. In the future, I plan to add other things onto the blog like lettering.js for custom blog headers and more experimental css3 simply for testing purposes.

AT A GLANCE

CLIENT
Personal Blog

PROJECT TYPE
Responsive Blog & CMS

TARGET DEVICES
Desktop / Mobile

VIEW PROJECT

DESIGN & DEVELOPMENT

Blog.manikrathee.com is my newly designed blog. The entire layout is a custom responsive wordpress build that I created as a "one hour project." I spent under an hour doing all of the layout, design, developement and testing. It is still in its infancy with less than ten posts but I plan to expand it with technical posts regarding responsive design and new css3/html5 techniques.

PROCESS

I have been taking on multiple short side projects from day to day, ranging from tumblr themes to wordpress sites. This blog, as stated above, was created in under one hour. It is built using the 1140gs, so it is responsive, html5 boiler, fit-text and multiple other jquery items. In the future, I plan to add other things onto the blog like lettering.js for custom blog headers and more experimental css3 simply for testing purposes.

MANIK RATHEE

GRACE DUONG
Graphic Designer

Grace Duong is a graphic designer from Philadelphia but has since relocated to Los Angeles. She is a recent graduate of the Tyler School of Art—Temple University where she went through the rigorous Graphic & Interactive Design ~~bootcamp~~ BFA program. She graduated with a 20-pound portfolio and a crooked spine. Just kidding. She has been named one of *CMYK* magazine's Top 100 New Creatives and was also selected to participate in the Art Director Club's National Student Portfolio Review. Grace looks forward to all future design adventures with a thirst to always learn, love and give the best efforts humanly possible.

Building My Own Brand

When I approached designing my identity, I wanted to design something that represented me and also stood out from the crowd. I was inspired by these circular Chinese motifs that I grew up seeing, and they also give homage to my culture. I wanted to incorporate balance in my identity, since I am constantly looking for balance not only in my work, but also in life. My logo is a half circle made of my initials that reflect one another. I also wanted to create a strong mark, one that would primarily be used in black to contrast with my work, since most of my work is colorful. Also, how perfect is it that my initials correlate with Graphic Design?

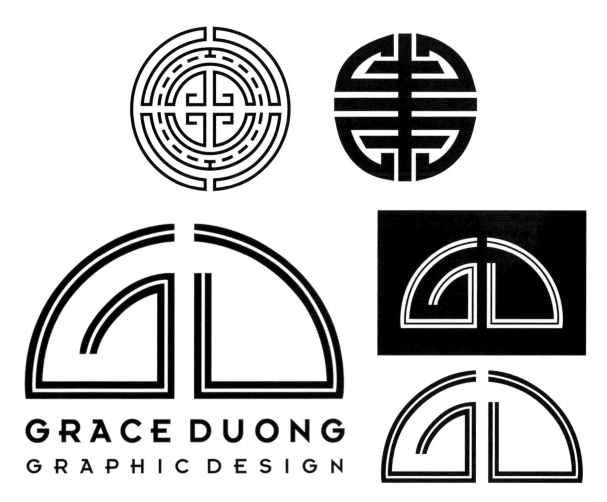

GRACE DUONG

MICHAEL SICKINGER
Creative Marketing, Givaudan

Michael is a guy's guy who lives for the thrill, disdains the dull and creates visual solutions that grab people's attention and keep it. An award-winning creative director/designer for print and screen-based media, Michael has been creating engaging brand experiences for nearly 15 years.

Over the course of his career, Michael has worked in a variety of settings—from ad agencies to fragrance and flavor companies.

During this time he has lent his creative insights to such clients as Reckitt Benckiser, Colgate-Palmolive, Procter and Gamble, The Coca-Cola Company, Pepsico, Snapple, AT&T and Harley Davidson. Currently Givaudan Fragrances is the place he calls home, where he works on some of the world's top fragrance brands.

Building My Own Brand

A personal identity should be a simple graphic that visually says something about the individual without being too literal. Being the kind of guy I am, I wanted to design an identity that was simple and clean, with an element of high energy. I chose a bold italic font with a drop shadow made up of angled lines to give the feeling of speed that is racing inspired.

Kelly Thorn
*Junior Designer,
Louise Fili Ltd.*

Kelly Thorn is currently living in Brooklyn, working as the junior designer at Louise Fili Ltd. and freelancing in her spare time. She specializes in hand lettering, typography, illustration and design, and is a recent graduate from Tyler School of Art-Temple University in Philadelphia.

Building My Own Brand

I chose to go about my branding the same way I choose to go about my life—friendly, unpretentious and fun. (Or so I'd like to think!) My concept for my visual identity is based on the very basic construction of letters, as I wanted it to speak to my lettering specialties. The colors I chose are simple yet effective, and easy to translate in different applications.

FROM *the* **DESK** *of* **KELLY THORN**

CONTACT
T 908 878 9720   E kellymthorn@gmail.com
W thornographicdesign.com

EDUCATION
Tyler School of Art of Temple University, Philadelphia, PA
BFA in Graphic & Interactive Design · Graduating Spring 2012

EMPLOYMENT
2012 – present · Junior Designer at Louise Fili, Ltd; New York City, NY
2012 – present · Assistant at International Typefounders, Inc; Lansdale, PA
2011 · Summer Intern at Hallmark Cards; Kansas City, MO
2010 · Body artist at Stacey's Face Painting, Philadelphia Zoo, PA
2009 – 2012 · Nanny; Bryn Mawr, PA

PUBLICATIONS
2012 · Little Book of Lettering; Rotovision and Chronicle Books
(to be published October 2012)
2012 · Applied Arts Student Awards issue
2011 · Work featured on WeLoveTypography.com, TypeEverything.com,
LovelyPackage.com, and DesignWorkLife.com
2010 · *From Here to There: A Curious Collection from the Hand Drawn
Map Association*; Princeton Architecture Press

RECOGNITION
2012 · Art Directors Club National Student Portfolio Review participant
2012 · Tyler School of Art Senior Show card winner
2011 · Applied Arts Student Awards winner
2010 · Honorable mention in Flux Student Design Competition
2010 · One Club Scholarship; chosen by GAID faculty members
2009 · Tyler School of Art Restaurant Identity Exhibition; 2nd place;
judged by Jessica Hische

EXHIBITIONS
2012 · Tyler School of Art GAID Senior Show
2011 · Hallmark's Annual Intern Portfolio Show
2011 · Tyler School of Art Packaging Show
2010 · Must Be Nice art show; Robinson's Urban Thrift, Philadelphia
2009 · Tyler School of Art Restaurant Identity Exhibition; Philadelphia
2009 · AIGA Campaign 2 Sustain juried poster competition; Philadelphia

SKILLS
Adobe CS 5.5: Photoshop, Illustrator, InDesign, Dreamweaver, After Effects,
and Flash · Fontlab Studio 5 · Illustration · Hand lettering · Type design

KELLY THORN

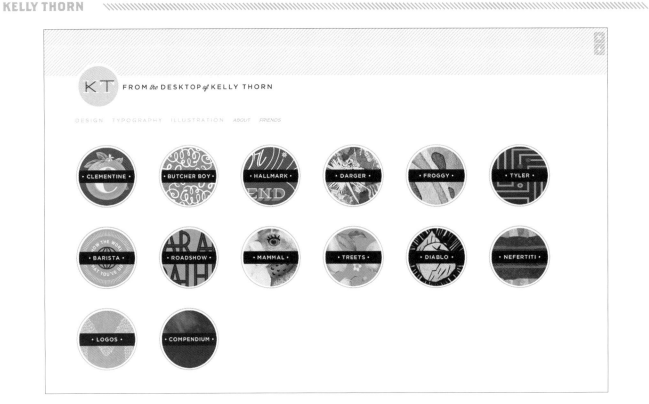

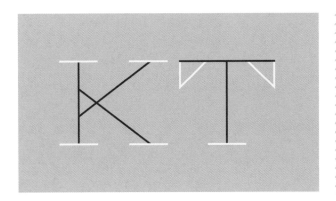

FROM *the* WALLET *of* KELLY THORN

- E kellymthorn@gmail.com
- W thornographicdesign.com
- T 908 878 9720

INVOICE FROM *the* **DESK** *of* **KELLY THORN**

My favorite client

DELIVERABLES
 A little bit of this · $123.00
 A little bit of that · $456.00

TOTAL
 $OME MONEY

JOBS ON DECK
 Birthday Card Illustration · est. 2 hours left · *finish by August*
 Wedding Invitation · *finish by end of July*

Thank you!
If you have any qualms or questions at all, please do not hesitate to contact me.

Kelly Thorn · July 24, 2012

Kenny Barela
Senior Art Director, The Integer Group

Kenny Barela is a creative industry professional with over eleven years of experience. He grew up in Santa Fe, New Mexico, where art and culture were a part of everyday life. Summers were always spent outdoors, hiking, camping and fly fishing—activities he is still very passionate about.

Early on in his career he co-founded and was creative director of a boutique design and creative agency in Albuquerque, New Mexico, called SUM. During his time at SUM, Kenny produced award-winning branding, interactive and big-idea solutions for businesses around the globe and even operated a three-year joint venture with a company in South America.

Now Kenny is living in Denver, Colorado, working as a senior art director at The Integer Group, one of the world's largest promotional, retail and shopper marketing agencies and part of the TBWA\ global agency network within Omnicom. Daily he strives to find that delicate balance between what looks good and what works—strategy + creativity.

Other things to know about Kenny:

- A bit of a collector (Have you seen the show *American Pickers*? Yeah, kind of like that.)
- Thinks he can still breakdance
- Can often be found scooting around town on his Genuine Stella scooter

Building My Own Brand

Simply, I wanted the self-promo to cleverly demonstrate who I am and what I believe about design and advertising—that winning ideas are based on both strategy and creativity. I thought a cool way of representing that would be to screen print a tie and pocket protector [to represent strategy] on a t-shirt [to represent creativity]. Plus, who doesn't like a cool free t-shirt! Also, culture is a big deal in the agency world. It has to be the right fit for both parties. It's not just about what you can do but also who you are. So, for demonstrating who I am, I wanted the viewer to see it, not read it. We're in the business of visual communication, after all. I decided an infographic would be the best tool to do that. On one sheet they could visually get to know me by seeing my likes and dislikes, hobbies and interests, personality, etc.

Overall, my motivation was that this was my best shot at getting behind closed doors and so it had to be the best representation of me since I couldn't be there physically—this was my brand. I also tried to put myself in the shoes of the talent manager, who no doubt sees dozens if not hundreds of résumés a week. What could I do to make their day and get them to want to meet me in person?

KENNY BARELA

About	Kenny is a visual communicator; a problem solver; a team player; an outdoor enthusiast.	
Employment	2004 - Present	**SUM Agency** Creative Director / Managing Partner
	2004 - 2005	**The Art Center Design College** Graphic Design and Website Design Instructor
	2003 - 2004	**Clear Channel Communications / Outdoor/ New Mexico** Creative Director
	2002 - 2003	**ABQ Arts Magazine** Art Director
	2001 - 2002	**Imagen Magazine** Art Director
	2000 - 2004	**Freelance Graphic Design**
Education	**The Art Center Design College - 1999 - 2002** Albuquerque, New Mexico Bachelor of Arts - Graphic Design	
	Santa Fe High School - 1994 - 1998 Santa Fe, New Mexico Diploma	

Skills

Specialities:
- Branding / Identity Design
- Creative / Art Direction
- Website Design
- Promotional Design
- Creative Copywriting
- Proposals & Presentations
- Corporate Collateral
- Social Media
- Publication Design
- Annual Reports
- Print & Prepress
- Photography

OS & Software:
- Mac OS
- Adobe Creative Suite (incl. Flash, Dreamweaver)
- Apple iWork
- Microsoft Word
- Microsoft Excel

Activities & Accolades

Board of Directors
Christina Kent Early Childhood Center (a 501(c)(3) non-profit) - 2007-2009

United Way of Central New Mexico
Monthly Donor

Pro Bono Services
Cystic Fibrosis Foundation; Active 20/30 Club of Albuquerque; Christina Kent

NM Ad Fed Addy Awards - Recognitions of Advertising and Design Excellence
Judges Choice Award, Multiple Gold Addys, Multiple Silver Addys - 2004-2008

References

Kenny demonstrates the utmost in creative application, ethics, integrity, and loyalty. His core values were reflected in his work and attitude every day. As our Creative Director, Kenny demonstrated an ability to get along and work closely with a strong and very dynamic and demanding sales team. He fit beautifully in the culture allowing us to deliver successful service and products to our clients.

I am happy to recommend Kenny for a position where an organization truly values the attributes aforementioned.

Sally Adams
President
Clear Channel Outdoor, NM
P 505 345 3589

I have had the pleasure of knowing Kenny Barela for more than seven years and have had the opportunity to work with him and his agency for various projects. Kenny's personal character, integrity and creative talent is outstanding and, having seen much of his recent work, I believe he has certainly continued to grow this professional gift.

Please consider this note as a personal reference for Kenny Barela as you consider his future employment.

Roger Hunter
National Marketing Coordinator
Faith Comes by Hearing
P 505 881 3321

I have worked with Kenny for over seven years. His creativity, execution, and knowledge are essential for any company. Not only is he one of the best in his field, he is full of integrity and value.

I would recommend him for any project or suitable position within your company.

Philip Ortiz
Corporate Communications
Wilson & Company
P 505 400 6426

Jim Godfrey
Designer and Chair of the Department of Art and Visual Communications, Utah Valley University

Jim Godfrey is a type junkie who finds himself comping type on his kids' sack lunches before they go to school. He is the chair of the department of art and visual communications at Utah Valley University and has been working with type for over twenty years. In a previous life, he was an art director and creative director at ad agencies in Salt Lake City and Montana, designing for Marker Ski Bindings, Yellowstone National Park and Sun Valley. In the next life, he hopes to be reincarnated as Claude Garamond. For some of his limited edition posters, log on to www.jimgodfreydesign.com.

Building My Own Brand

As a self-described type junkie, it is only fitting that my personal brand identity revolves around typography. From my logo to web posts to products for sale, I make everything relate in some way to typography.

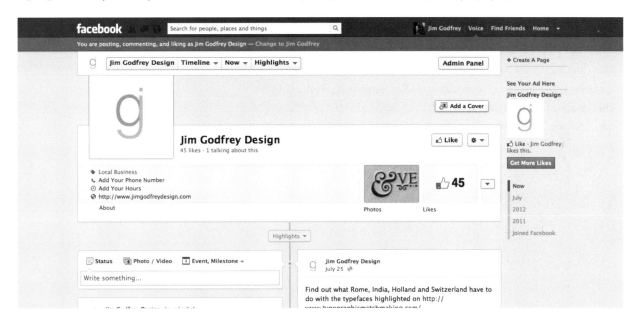

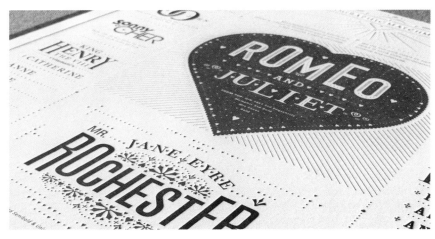

JIM GODFREY

thirty-four Typographic Sins

1. **Two spaces between sentences.**
   Repent of this sin by using only one space.

2. **Dumb quotes instead of smart quotes.**
   Evil: "Thou shalt not misuse type" § Good: "Thou shalt not misuse type".

3. **Dumb apostrophe instead of a smart apostrophe.**
   Profane: Don't use prime marks § Sacred: Don't use prime marks By the way, apostrophes always face this way. Pot 'o' gold. They never face this way. Pot 'o gold.

4. **Failing to tuck periods/commas inside quote marks.**
   Immoral: "I love type so much", she continued. Chaste: "I love type so much," she testified.

5. **Failing to kern display type.**
   Unseemly gaps can impede readability and be distracting to the reader. Adjusting the spacing between letters will assuage your guilt.

6. **Using a hyphen instead of an en dash.**
   Use an en dash to indicate a duration of time instead of the word "to", the 8–10 commandments, not 8–10 commandments.

7. **Using two hyphens instead of an em dash.**
   An em dash signifies a change in thought—or a parenthetical phrase—within a sentence.

8. **Too many consecutive hyphens.**
   It is sinful to have more than two hyphens on consecutive lines of type, and even that should be avoided.

9. **Large amounts of bodytext in uppercase letters.**
   IT BECOMES REALLY DIFFICULT TO READ

10. **Large amounts of reversed type**
    ARE HARDER TO READ. *Type on a busy background is also unreadable.*

11. **Using process colors for body text.**
    It is harder to read, but more importantly, it is hell to register on press.

12. **Underlining titles instead of italicizing them.**
    Thou Shalt Not: <u>The Holy Bible</u> Thou Shalt: *The Koran*

13. **Failing to eliminate widows.**
    A widow is a word that sits on a line by itself at the end of a paragraph. Avoid this or risk being cast into a lake of fire and brimstone.

14. **Failing to eliminate orphans.**
    An orphan is the last line of a paragraph that sits alone at the top of a column or page. Type does not like to be alone.

15. **Rivers in justified text.**
    Unsightly large spaces between words occur if the line length is too short or the point size of the text too large.

16. **Inconsistent leading.**
    Paragraphs should have the same leading for each line.

17. **Indenting the first paragraph.**
    The first paragraph is never indented, subsequent paragraphs are.

18. **Indenting a paragraph too far.**
    The standard indent for a paragraph is 1 em, not ½ inch. Most software has default tabs set for ½ inch, so adjust the tabs.

19. **Failing to hang punctuation into the margin.**
    Punctuation has less visual weight than letters or numbers. Compensate for this in display text by hanging the punctuation into the margin.

20. **Failing to use or create fractions.**
    Wicked: 1/2 § Righteous: ½

21. **Incorrectly abbreviating AM and PM.**
    Unclean: am, AM, A.M. § Relatively Clean: a.m. § Clean: a.m. or AM

22. **Failing to provide margins for type in a box.**
    ugly   beautiful

23. **Faux italic/oblique, bold and small cap type.**
    Impure: Italic § Pure: Italic
    *Sinful: **Bold** § Virtuous: **Bold***
    Unkosher: SMALLCAPS § Kosher: SMALLCAPS

24. **Strokes that encroach upon letterforms.**
    Hellacious § Heavenly

25. **Horizontally scaled type.**
    Unrepentant: Scaled. § Penitent: A condensed typeface

26. **Vertically scaled type.**
    Purgatory: Scaled. § Heaven: An extended typeface

27. **Negative letterspacing.**
    Not very readable.

28. **Bad line breaks in headlines and body text.**
    If you don't break lines for sense, they can be harder to read.

29. **Stacking lowercase letters.**
    Vertical baselines are celestial.

30. **Failing to indent bulleted lists.**
    • *Bulleted lists look better when the second line aligns flush with the first letter of the line above it, instead of with the bullet.*

31. **Failing to use accent marks.**
    Sinner: No esta aqui. § Saint: No está aquí.

32. **Failing to align baselines of type in adjacent columns of body text.**
    Baselines of all columns of text on a page should align. This creates a pleasing margin of gutter white space.

33. **Failing to correct bad rags.**
    For centered or non-justified text, avoid obvious shapes (like pyramids, steps, wedges, singles and overly short or long lines).

34. **Failing to use ligatures.**
    unholy: finish § holy: finish

Jon Contino

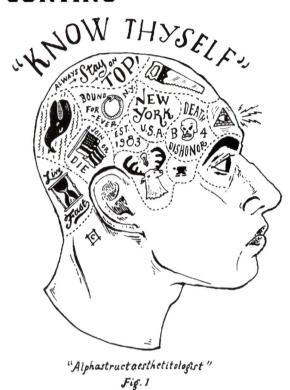

"Alphastructaesthetitologist"
Fig. 1

Building My Own Brand

Creating a personal identity has always been something that's plagued me. In fact, I don't think I've ever heard another designer say otherwise. It's one of the toughest things to do. Normally you're taking the concept of a company and breaking it down into simple little pictures, but in the case of self-branding, you need to critique and comment on yourself in one simple mark. How do you summarize your entire life with that one mark?! The concept for my personal branding came out of a pure "who cares" attitude. I was doodling one day while watching a Yankees game and sketched a baseball with the words "New York" on the top and bottom, and "Yankees" stretching across the middle. I had seen similar designs plenty of times before, but I was getting a good vibe from this. Once I finally sat down, I played with it a bit and came up with something completely nonsensical and yet completely right. The same concept of a baseball, except with all my junk in there instead.

Once I had the mark down, I decided on using a dark navy and yellow gold to define the color of my brand. This palette is based on the old New York state license plates I had loved so much as a kid, and as such, represented everything I remembered from my childhood, but with a sense of history and persistence that comes along with being born in one of the original 13 [colonies]. From there, I began developing minor alternate marks here and there, all with similar histories, and I'm able to use them each for different and unique purposes while still maintaining that semblance of a united brand identity.

JON CONTINO

JON CONTINO

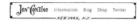

Information Blog Shop Twitter

"The demand for his services speaks to the creativity and ingenuity of his work, and to a vague yet persistent hunger for the tactile in modern American culture."

— Ben Bishop, Ragged Band

As a New York native, Jon Contino has been under the influence of corporate mass marketing and inspirational street art since his first breath. Not surprisingly, he has garnered considerable attention for his unique approach to design utilizing hand-drawn lettering and typographic illustration in conjunction with a modern, yet minimalistic sensibility.

He has received numerous accolades for his fusion of old and new world aesthetics and continues to influence modern trends in graphic design and apparel design.

Jon resides in Brooklyn with his wife Erin where he works not only as a freelance illustrator, but also as Co-Founder and Creative Director of menswear brand CXXVI Clothing Company.

He is currently accepting new commissions. For all inquiries regarding consulting, speaking engagements, or workshops, please email for further information.

NEW BUSINESS
Ben Arditti
ben@satelliteoffice.tv
1 (773) 818-4438

DIRECT
joncontino@gmail.com
Twitter: @joncontino
Instagram: @joncontino
LinkedIn: Profile
Facebook: Profile

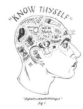

RECENT FEATURES
Dribbble Time Out
Ragged Band
The Creative Insight
ADC Young Guns 9 Award
Designs
The Fox is Black & Contribution
Momentus Project
Daily Drop Cap
Designers MX
Friends of Type
The Artful

RECENT HONORS
Art Directors Club Young Guns 9 Winner
American Illustration 31 Award
2011 AAF Seattle ADDY Award
2011 Comm Arts Typography Annual
2011 Denver 50 Award in Adv. and Design
DSVC Professional Show Judge

BOOKS & PUBLICATIONS
Stickerbomb Letters, 2012
Reinventing Lettering, 2012
Introducing: Visual Identities..., 2012
Los Logos 6, 2012
Codex: Issue 1, 2011
TypoShirt One, 2010
New Ornamental Type, 2010
Lettering: Beyond Computer Graphics, 2009
TEES: The Art of the T-Shirt, 2009

SELECT PRESS
Communication Arts Typography Annual, GQ, Grain Edit, Codex, New York Magazine, NBC New York, The Fox is Black, Inc. Magazine, Lürzer's Archive, Nylon Guys, Form Fifty Five, Lettercult, HOW Magazine, It's Nice That, Los Angeles Times, Computer Arts Projects, Antenna Magazine, Uncrate, Hypebeast

SELECT CLIENTS
Coca-Cola, Nike, Random House, AT&T, General Electric, Kellogg's, The New York Times, Rachel Ray, New Balance, The Washington Post, Harper Collins, ESPN, Wired Magazine, Matix Clothing, Camel, Ogilvy & Mather, FX Networks, Leo Burnett, Obey Clothing, Publix Super Markets, Sterling Publishing, Element Skateboards, La Marzocco, AICA, Little Brown and Company, Billykirk, Washington State Lottery, Victoria's Secret

All works copyright © 2012 Jon Contino.
Do not reproduce without permission.

JON CONTINO

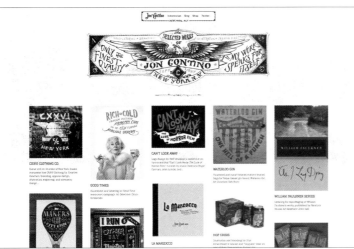

Allison Kerek
Hallmark Cards

I always knew that I wanted to be an artist. As a younger, tinier Allison, I watched cartoons that were way too inappropriate for me, such as *Beavis and Butthead*, *South Park* and *Ren and Stimpy*. As I watched these bizarre animations, I was certain that I would grow to be some sort of creator. I grew up in Lancaster, Pennsylvania, where a decent artistic community existed. Entering art school was always the plan. I decided to move to Philadelphia and attend Tyler School of Art, which was the best decision that I've ever made. Tyler had an extremely competitive graphic design program, which always kept me on my toes and pushed me to my reach my full potential. I was very lucky to have had the chance to live in Philadelphia. I hated it at first, but grew to love it. It's such an insane, trashy, artistic, historic, disgusting and beautiful city… which inspired me deeply.

After graduating from Tyler at the top of my class, I was recruited by Hallmark and moved to Kansas City, Missouri. While I do miss Philly, I enjoy my new job, and love that I have the freedom to leave work at 5:00 P.M. and go home to create my own illustrations. I might return to the East Coast at some point, but for now I am happy.

Building My Own Brand

When it came to building my brand, one thing was obvious: It had to be hand done. I wanted my brand to show off my illustration style and to clarify that I produce my work by hand. With this in mind, I created a self-portrait with my name underneath and the title "Illustrator-Designer-Animator." This would let everyone know who I am, what I do and how I do it.

When I was creating my résumé, I debated whether I wanted to make it kind of wild like my illustrations or to have it more clean and to the point for legibility purposes. I went with the second option since I wanted the viewer to be able to pinpoint my information right away. In the future, I might create a more densely illustrated résumé, but for now I am very pleased with how this one turned out.

Creating my website was my favorite part of building my brand. I decided to put all information at the top, clarifying whose work you are looking at. Then I made fun icons with hand-done titles for each of my projects and separated them into the groups: design, animation and web.

The icons were taken directly from the projects that I designed. I created them with the intention that they would be a sneak preview of what you were about to look at. I built my website on Cargo Collective, which I highly recommend for anyone who is about to make a personal website. It's easy to use and looks great.

ALLISON KEREK
ILLUSTRATION → DESIGN → ANIMATION

✉ CONTACT
YOU can CALL ME at (717) 951.2158
SNAIL MAIL goes to → 2425 E. CUMBERLAND ST.
PHILADELPHIA, PA, 19125
EMAIL ME at → ALLISONKEREK@GMAIL.com
CHECK ME OUT here → www.ALLISONKEREK.com

👁 EMPLOYMENT
2012-PRESENT → HALLMARK CARDS
KANSAS CITY, MISSOURI, GRAPHIC DESIGNER
2009-2011 → STACEY'S FACE PAINTING
PHILADELPHIA, PENNSYLVANIA, BODY ARTIST

🎓 EDUCATION
TYLER SCHOOL of ART → 2012
BFA in GRAPHIC and INTERACTIVE DESIGN

👁 SKILLS
ADOBE 5.5 → CREATIVE SUITE
PRINT MAKING → ETCHING and SERIGRAPHY

★ EXHIBITIONS
2012 → THE ONE CLUB 18th ANNUAL STUDENT EXHIBITION
ONE CLUB GALLERY, NEW YORK
2012 → SENIOR SHOW → TYLER SCHOOL of ART
2011 → PACKAGING SHOW → TYLER SCHOOL of ART
2010 → MUST BE NICE → URBAN THRIFT STORE
2009 → RESTAURANT SHOW → TYLER SCHOOL of ART

🏆 AWARDS
2012 → TYLER SCHOOL of ART TOP PORTFOLIO
2012 → APPLIED ARTS STUDENT AWARDS ISSUE
2012 → HOW MAGAZINE SELF PROMOTION ISSUE
2012 → TYLER SCHOOL of ART FACULTY AWARD
BEST ILLUSTRATION AWARD/ BEST ANIMATION AWARD
2012 → TYLER SCHOOL of ART INTERACT 10
BEST ANIMATION AWARD/ BEST IN SHOW
2012 → ART DIRECTORS CLUB in NEW YORK CITY
NATIONAL STUDENT PORTFOLIO REVIEW PARTICIPANT
2010 → AIGA FLUX 2010 → POSTER AWARD
2009 → BANNER COMPETITION → 1st PLACE
TYLER SCHOOL of ART

● CLIENTS
LIGHTNINGING → PHILADELPHIA BAND
DJ DEF JANIELS → PHILADELPHIA DJ
STRAWBERRY HILL → LANCASTER RESTAURANT

ALLISON KEREK

Gui Borchert
Creative Director, 72andSunny

Gui Borchert is a creative director with a background in art direction and design. He doesn't believe in the separation between traditional and digital campaigns and believes great ideas can live anywhere.

Borchert is currently a Creative Director at 72andSunny. He just moved to LA from London where he was a Creative Director at Fallon for two years.

He has been the Creative Director on PUMA Football at Syrup New York, and has worked at Mother New York and R/GA. He's worked on such brands as Nike, Cadbury, Nokia, Johnson & Johnson, Absolut, New Balance, and many others.

His interests include football (soccer) among many other things not as interesting as football (soccer).

Building My Own Brand

I prefer not to look at it as "branding" and more like an extension of who I am. My work is versatile—I like to transition between different looks, styles, things—and I think that comes across in the way I treat my personal identity. Most importantly, it's almost as if I don't really think too much about it. It just comes naturally, and I believe that's the best way to do it—more authentic and less calculated.

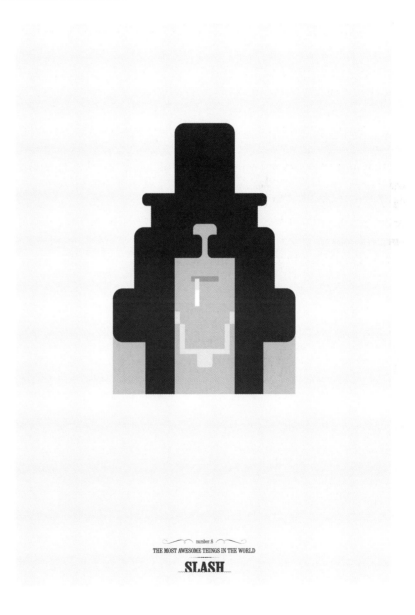

number 8
THE MOST AWESOME THINGS IN THE WORLD
SLASH

GUI BORCHERT
Orange Popcorn Campaign
Film, Fresh!
Orange Phoneheads
Film, Fresh!
Orange Tiny Top-Ups TV Spot
Film, Fresh!
Puma Make Football Anywhere
Print, Fresh!
Puma World Cup TV Spot
Film, Fresh!
Puma Museum of Power
Interactive, Fresh!
Puma Football Event Posters
Design, Print, Fresh!
Puma Lightning Boot
Print, Fresh!
Puma Love Equals Football
Integrated, Print, Film
Puma Power of Football
Print, Integrated, Fresh!
Stefan Sagmeister Illustration
Design
Puma WPS 2011
Film, Print, Fresh!
Puma Manchester Rain
Print, Fresh!
Type Texturizer
Interactive, Design, Fresh!
Puma Football Speed
Print, Film, Fresh!
Nike Restoration
Print, Interactive, Fresh!
Artists for Obama Poster
Design, Fresh!
MTV Brasil
Design
Nike Beautiful
Film, Fresh!
Nike Considered
Print, Interactive
SACC Green Invite
Design, Fresh!
Dell Faces
Film
Recon Operation 6453
Mobile, Interactive, Integrated
NYC 2012 Logo Proposal
Design, Fresh!
Puma Ligue 1 Ball
Print, Film, Fresh!
Nikelab
Interactive
Absolut Vodka Brasil Bottle
Design, Fresh!
Puma WPS 2010
Film, Print
Gamepro Splinter Cell Cover
Design
Puma Farewell
Film
Dell Summer Rocks Identity
Design
Nike Plus
Interactive, Integrated, Mobile
Nokia + R/GA Mobile Data
Film
MTVs Promo
Interactive
Nike Evolution Posters
Print
Nikelab Design by Nature
Interactive, Fresh!
R/GA Origami Holiday Card
Interactive
Greenpeace Oceans Awareness
Design, Print
Newsweek Cover
Design
Nike Air Max 360
Film, Interactive, Fresh!
Nike Free
Interactive
LVHRD Poster
Design
Nike Zoom Robinho
Film
Popeyes Love That Chicken Poster
Print
NikeiD Website
Interactive
Letter K for Spelling Change
Design
Nike Vapor Series
Film, Print, Integrated
Dell Out of Home
Print
Artism - Art for Autism
Design
Disorder In Progress Book
Design
Dell Wheelman
Print
Nike Art of Speed
Film, Interactive, Fresh!
Gworka Pixel Art Playground
Interactive
Nike Running Made Better
Interactive
Pixel Art Illustrations
Design
Open Colony Full Branding
Design, Interactive
Nikelab Dreams of Motion
Interactive
Rembrandt Print Campaign
Print
Coke Promo Style Frames
Design
Puma WPS 2009
Print, Film
Sign Cafe Magazine
Design
Nike Earth
Interactive, Mobile, Integrated
R/GA Sculptures Holiday Card
Interactive
Nike Mayfly Poster
Print
Visual Experiments
Design
Website Archive
Interactive
Logo Collection
Design

GUI BORCHERT

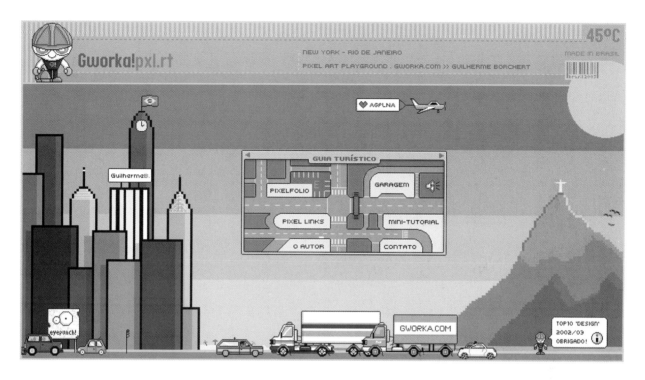

Above: Gworka.com: personal website, 2001
Left: Among the Monkeys: experiment, 2002

GUI BORCHERT

Visual experiment, mixed media, 2009

GUI BORCHERT

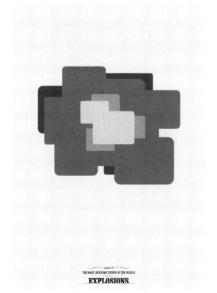

The Most Awesome Things in the World: poster series, 2012.

CHAPTER FIVE
RESOURCES

COLOR

In the past and even today, color symbolism in fine art, religious rituals and ceremonies, literature and fashion is not universal. It is specific to cultures, religions and countries. In some ways, the use of color in graphic design has globalized color—through brand association and color-coded cues in package design. For example, Coca-Cola is associated with a specific red; if you visit the brand's websites in various countries, such as the United States, Botswana and Japan, you'll see that red used on those websites. (See http://www.coca-cola.com/en/index.html; http://www.coca-cola.com/bo/pages/landing/index.html; http://www.cocacola.jp/.)

In food package design, for instance, green often denotes "organic," or red-violet may denote raspberry flavor. Certain color combinations are easier to read on-screen and in print, which influences color palette choices. This isn't an issue in fine art or fashion or color used in religious rituals. The worldwide ubiquity of graphic design solutions has certainly affected how we understand color.

How color is utilized symbolically across cultures is a study in itself. For example, how each country in Africa utilizes and characterizes red is an extensive and fascinating study alone. If we think about how people made colors five hundred years ago—where they found them in nature and the rarity of certain colors available for making dyes and paint pigments—then we can understand some of the associations, as well.

This reference scratches the surface of color symbolism. Please view it as a sample to entice you to research further. (For some fascinating history, read, *Colors: What They Mean and How to Make Them* by Anne Varichon [Harry N. Abrams, 2007].)

In North America, graphic designers feel free to use color and construct color palettes as they wish, for the most part. In package design, color is often a cue to flavor or scent. For example, yellow signifies lemon scented or citrus flavor. National holidays, holidays and religious holidays popular in the United States are denoted by color and color palettes. For example, the colors of the American flag are used on Independence Day, July 4th; orange and black are used for Halloween; and red and green are used for Christmas. Also, many national brands "own" a color.

For your personal brand, of course, feel free to experiment without taking ancient meanings to heart, but do research color symbolism related to a specific audience as well as conventional graphic design color cues.

Below are some common associations Americans make with colors:

- **Gender:** Pink denotes baby girls; blue denotes baby boys; yellow and green are gender neutral
- **Clean:** Green and blue are considered clean; green also can mean recycled or sustainable materials or processes
- **Purity:** White and blue
- **Luxury:** Gold, silver and metallic
- **Cool:** Green denotes menthol flavor or mint
- **Diversity:** Rainbow

GLOSSARY OF COLORS

Black is a neutral and one of the first color terms found in ancient languages. Primitive man likely associated black with night and the unknown recesses of caves and deep forests. In literature and film, black became associated with mystery, death—and in the Western film genre, with the "bad guys." Coco Chanel changed modern fashion's point of view in the 1920s, with the sophistication of the little black dress, and black still reigns supreme as a symbol of pared-down sophistication. In Western countries, black is the color of mourning. Associated with individuality and trendsetters, black is worn by artists and designers. It is also associated with rebellion, as represented by a black leather jacket like the one Marlon Brando wore in *The Wild One*.

White is also one of the first color-related terms in language, going back to an Indo-European root. In Western art, literature and film, white has come to symbolize light, purity and in the Western film genre, the "good guys." Also in some Western cultures, brides wear white. White is associated with cleanliness; health care professionals wear white and many bed linens are white. For people in snowy climates, *white* is an important word. White is also associated with innocence. In war, a white flag is a sign of surrender or truce.

Red is a primary color on the pigment color wheel; a true red, fully saturated, is a visually hot color. From natural associations, it represents fire, heat, the heart and blood (life, death, fertility, transformations, female puberty, danger, cures, and hunting). Interestingly, within Western art and literature, red is associated with very different concepts—love (relating to the human heart) and seduction and passion, as well as with anger, evil (the Devil is often depicted in red) and danger (perhaps danger isn't that different than passion). Similar to blood and wounds, red also is related to the idea of courage, as exemplified in the novel, *The Red Badge of Courage* by Stephen Crane. In many cultures, red plays a role in ceremonies and rituals, from engagement to marriage to war. For example, in India, red plays a significant role in the wedding ceremony. In many armies around the world, past and present, red is one of the colors of military uniforms. As an idiom, "in the red" denotes debts or losses on a financial balance sheet and the "red carpet" in American pop culture is a symbol of power and glamour. Due to the (RED) Campaign and red ribbon symbol, red is associated with fighting the worldwide AIDS epidemic. Due to its hot color temperature, it may also be seen as a color of strength, attracting people's attention. In China and most of Asia, red symbolizes prosperity and happiness. Also in China, red represents revitalization associated with the pomegranate fruit.

Orange is a secondary color on the pigment color wheel; a true orange, fully saturated, is a visually hot color.

From natural associations, it represents autumn (leaves turning color), heat of the sun, sunset, citrus fruit, flowers, spices. Red reminds us of the desert, rock or clay. Symbolically, related to nature and autumn, orange can symbolize change. Also related to citrus and the sun, orange symbolizes health and energy. In Western culture, orange is viewed as more playful than red, friendlier.

Yellow is a primary color on the pigment color wheel; a true yellow, fully saturated, is a visually hot color. From natural associations such as the sun, flowers, honey, sulphur, fruit and plants (for example, turmeric), it represents sunshine, brilliance, ripeness, springtime and new beginnings. However, muted yellows can also represent autumn, biliousness and weathering. Yellow has many contrary associations if you compare cultures, and even within cultures. In American modern culture, yellow can represent sunshine or cowardice or hope (as in the yellow ribbon symbolizing the hope of returning soldiers). In soccer, referees use yellow cards to communicate caution and offenses. At times, the associated meanings have to do with the saturation or yellow hue (lemon yellow versus saffron orange-yellow versus golden yellow versus turmeric yellow). Yellow is associated with Buddhism in the East. In Polynesia, yellow is divine. In Egypt, yellow signifies mourning.

Blue is a primary color on the pigment color wheel; blue is a visually cool color. Blue pigment is rare in nature. From natural associations, it represents coolness (water) and calm (water and sky). In Western art, from the twelfth century through the High Renaissance (and until today), blue became a coveted and popular color. In Italy, during the end of the Middle Ages and throughout the Renaissance, blue was associated with the Virgin Mary. Royals and the aristocracy showed interest in blue as well during those periods. In the United States, blue has several associative meanings: It is used to express melancholia, evidenced in a phrase "having the blues"; it is associated with the pensive saturnine tone of Picasso's Blue Period; and it even refers to an American music genre with African roots, "the blues" to mean music "marked by recurrent minor intervals."

Green is a secondary color; true green is a visually cool color. From natural associations with flora and fauna, it represents nature and renewal. In Ancient Egypt, green held positive meanings associated with growth and plant renewal. In hieroglyphics, a sprouting papyrus represented green. In Africa, green is also a positive color. For the Ndunga of the Congo, green is a symbol of nourishment. Green represents vitality in Ghana. Green is symbolic of Islam. In Celtic myth, the god of fertility is green. For many Native American cultures, green has a positive association with growth and fertile ground. In the United States, green has a number of associations, from money to being naïve to being green with envy, and most recently with sustainability, as in green design.

Violet (Purple) is a secondary color on the pigment color wheel; a true violet is a visually cool color. From natural associations with flora, it represents spring. As far as we can tell from discoveries about dyeing cloth, purple was used for kings, priests and other nobles. In Thailand, purple is the color of mourning for widows. Dark purples are traditionally associated with wealth and royalty, while lighter purples (like lavender) are considered more romantic.

Brown is a neutral that can have a cast of a dominant hue, such as red or orange or yellow. From natural associations, it represents the earth and its matter, such as wood and stone, and the richness and warmth of coffee and chocolate.

GLOSSARY OF SYMBOLS

Apple: In Western tradition, the apple has both positive and negative meanings; it became associated with knowledge and with temptation and sin (from Christianity, the forbidden fruit). In Greek mythology, Hippomenes uses three golden apples to distract the huntress Atalanta in a footrace to win her hand in marriage.

American Alligator: In contemporary culture, the American alligator is associated with opportunists. It symbolizes the nature of a predator but also a survivor since it managed to avoid extinction.

Bengal Tiger: In India, the Bengal tiger is the national animal and a key figure in lore. The tiger symbolizes both strength and agility and is associated with fearsomeness.

Cat (domestic): Early Egyptians worshipped a cat goddess. Cats are associated with nimbleness and agility, the night (they can see well at night) and aloofness.

Dogs: Domestic dogs are symbols of companionship and are known as "man's best friend." (They were probably the first animals to be tamed.) They are also associated with loyalty, bravery and rescue.

Bottlenose Dolphin: The dolphin can symbolize intelligence (they can be trained to perform) and friendliness, because their curved mouths look like a smile. The Ganges River Dolphin, or Susu, is the national aquatic animal of India.

Flowers: Flora, associated with spring and beauty. In vanitas paintings, cut flowers symbolize the transience of life.

Giant Panda: These rare pandas from China are solitary creatures and are associated with elusiveness. In contemporary life, the panda is associated with endangered species.

Grapevine: In Greek mythology, the vine is an attribute of Bacchus, the god of wine, and his followers. In general, a grapevine can mean fruitfulness or growth.

Golden Eagle: The eagle has several key associations, including swiftness and strength, and is a bird of prey. The golden eagle is the national bird of Mexico.

Horse: In most cultures, horses are honored creatures, linked to survival, work, war, the bond between animal and humans, and transportation. Horses are also associated with grace, beauty, speed and mercy.

King Cobra: Most often, snakes are associated with evil and venom. The king cobra is the longest of venomous snakes. In Freudian psychology and literature, the snake can be a phallic symbol.

Laurel: In Greek mythology, the laurel is associated with Apollo. In the arts, it is associated with poets, and in literature, it is a symbol of triumph.

Lotus: The lotus is the national flower of India. In the art and mythology of ancient India, the lotus is a sacred flower. In general, the lotus is associated with birth, creation and grace.

Monarch Butterfly: The butterfly is elusive and opulent and often considered carefree. The butterfly is key in a famous Chinese parable: Zhuangzi's dream of a butterfly. Zhuangzi, a legendary sage, dreams he is a yellow butterfly. However, upon awakening, he is unsure if he, Zhuangzi, dreamed he was a butterfly, or a butterfly dreamed he was Zhuangzi.

Peacock: Because females choose their mates according to the quality of the feather train, this bird is associated with courtship and attractiveness. It is the national bird of India.

Peony: In the East Asian pictorial canon, the peony is associated with feminine beauty and with prosperity.

Rose: In modern culture, red roses are associated with love and passion, yellow roses with friendship and white roses with purity.

Tiger: In Western cultures, the tiger has different meanings, including a passionate man or a man with erotic desires and ferociousness. It may be associated with the Greek god Bacchus. In Eastern cultures, the tiger is a venerable creature.

Tree: In Western art and literature, a tree can mean birth, rebirth (deciduous tree), redemption or a connection between earth and sky. It is related to death when depicted without leaves, damaged or fallen. In India, the fig tree represents immortality.

Wolves: Sometimes viewed as villains, wolves are most often associated with the hierarchy of a pack and roaming. They also have a positive association with fierce independence.

VISUALIZATION TECHNIQUES

One of the marvelous aspects of looking at drawings is that you can sense the person creating each; you can sense the movement of the artist's hand. The very essence of that momentary feeling is what makes drawing a very personal way to visually communicate. By trying a variety of strokes in the process of exploring visualization, you could well discover a new path for your personal identity.

Geometricize

Method: Geometricize the whole form, breaking the form into cubic shapes composed of triangles, pyramids, cones and cubes.

Goal: To simplify, yet render a volumetric form cubically

Model for this method: Luca Cambiaso (Italian, 1527–1585)

During the mid-1560s, as a quick drawing method, Cambiaso began visualizing with simplified cubic shapes. (http://www.liverpoolmuseums.org.uk/walker/collections/paperWorks/Cambiaso.aspx)

Clusters of Marks

Method: Create forms and shapes with clusters of parallel marks. Jeffrey Cudlin referred to marks drawn by artist Dan Flavin as, "odd cuneiform symbols or bundles of sticks." (Jeffrey Cudlin, http://www.washingtoncitypaper.com/articles/29667/reflected-glory)

Goal: To create bundles of form, bales of parallel marks that can stand alone or be combined.

Model for this method: Dan Flavin (American, 1933–1996), famous for his fluorescent light installations/sculptures, was a prolific draftsman who utilized a wide range of visualizing methods. In 1968, Flavin executed preparatory sketches in "scratchy" ballpoint pen for several "monuments" to the Russian artist Vladimir Tatlin.

Automatism

Method: Utilize automatic drawing—sketching without conscious thought given to the drawing itself—to create entire images or parts of images. In the visual arts, automatism often involves techniques for generating images that arise from chance-based components, such as *grattage* (scraping the inked or painted surface) and *frottage* (rubbing with graphite or crayon over grained or other textured surfaces).

Goal: To draw without reason or involve chance in the creation of the work

Models for this method: André Masson (French, 1896–1987) and doodlers everywhere

(http://www.moma.org/collection/browse_results.php?criteria=O%3AAD%3AE%3A3821&page_number=4&template_id=1&sort_order=1)

Automatic Drawing + Writing

Method: Utilize automatic drawing in combination with writing without conscious thought given to the drawing and writing themselves to create entire images or parts of images and written content.

Goal: To draw and write without reason or involve chance in the creation of the work

Models for this method:

- les Automatistes, a group of Canadian Surrealist painters, painted in a technique based on automatic writing
- Tachists (Hans Hartung, Gérard Schneider, Pierre Soulages, Frans Wols, Zao Wu-ki and Georges Mathieu)
- Chitra Ganesh (Brooklyn, New York, b. 1975)

The process of automatic writing is central to Ganesh's practice. To learn about Ganesh's work, visit http://www.chitraganesh.com/work.html.

Continuously Looping Lines

Method: Use continuous lines that swirl and loop around, repeating the lines to describe form, space and air simultaneously.

Goal: Create the illusion of volume and atmosphere simultaneously

Model for this method: Alberto Giacometti (Swiss, 1901–1966), sculptor, painter, draftsman and printmaker

Valerie J. Fletcher, senior curator of Modern Art at the Smithsonian, describes Giacometti's drawings of the post World War II period: "His drawing style consisted of rapidly executed, often continuous lines that swirl around, over, and through his subject, never quite defining it yet conveying a sense of its mass and mystery." (http://www.moma.org/m/explore/collection/art_terms/2141/0/1.iphone_ajax?klass=artist) To see Giacometti's drawings visit http://www.moma.org/collection/artist.php?artist_id=2141.

Collage Painting

Method: Using a variety of papers and fabrics, from found papers (wrapping paper, wall paper, cloth) to commercially produced colored papers and printed materials, create a collage. Then alter the surface by any means, for example, abrade the surface with sandpaper, remove color with erasers, draw or paint over areas. Add linear details with ink or graphite or other drawing materials.

Goal: Altering the surface properties to create a tactile quality with variety

Model for Method: Romare Bearden used a huge variety of papers and patterned fabrics for his collages. An "…important facet of his practice involved altering the surfaces of these papers and other collage elements in a variety of ways: adding painted areas using both spray paint and the more traditional brushed application of color; using abrasion and sanding to roughen and interrupt the plane; and removing color from both painted areas and collage papers by means of a bleaching agent." (www.nga.gov/feature/bearden/tech3.shtm)

Reductive Line

Method: Describe forms using a reductive linear drawing technique; no shading, but line can be descriptive.

Goal: Use line to efficiently describe form, with an emphasis on contour and overlaps for depth

Model for Method: Painter Ellsworth Kelly (American, b. 1923) relies on line to describe volume. He has drawn contours of plants—a thin efficient stroke creates each leaf, stem and flower. He does not use shading.

"His drawings are reductive—whole stems are sometimes omitted—but they are also uncannily descriptive. In the absence of shadows, overlaps become especially significant as indicators of depth," writes Karen Rosenberg in *The New York Times*, describing Ellsworth Kelly's plant drawings at the Metropolitan Museum of Art in New York.

(http://www.nytimes.com/2012/06/08/arts/design/ellsworth-kellys-plant-drawings-at-the-met.html)

Patterns of Dots

Method: Utilize and vary and repeat fields of (very small to medium to large) dots and webs of slug-shaped strokes, and mix with linear elements as well as small triangular elements and constellations of lines.

Goal: To create the illusion of form and space using polka dots, draw fields of dots of varying sizes, clusters of lines, slug-shaped strokes and small forms embedded in other forms to create patterns

Model for Method: Yayoi Kusama (Japanese, b. 1929) is a sculptor, painter and novelist. She is perhaps best known for her use of polka dots and nets as motifs, which she started to use at the age of ten.

Many of Kusama's abstract yet detailed drawings from the early 1950s were done in ink, watercolor, pastel and collage, and they referenced animals, cellular and botanical forms. In *The New York Times*, Holland Cotter described some on exhibit at the Whitney Museum of American Art, as "…the sum of repeated, labor-intensive details: fields of minute dots, clusters of radiant lines, networks of slug-shaped strokes." *(http://www.nytimes.com/2012/07/13/arts/design/yayoi-kusama-at-whitney-museum-of-american-art.html?pagewanted=all)*

To see Kasuma's work, visit http://www.yayoi-kusama.jp.

Decalcomania

Method: Apply ink or paint to a piece of paper that is then pressed against another sheet of paper, transferring an accidental image and resulting in a fractal pattern. Or, apply ink or paint to a piece of paper (usually at the midline of the page), then fold the paper in half to create a mirrored pattern, a kind of Rorschach blot. Elaborate on the resulting image.

Goal: To elaborate through deliberation on an image made by chance, an interplay between forces of chance and design

Model for Method: Surrealist artist Oscar Domínguez (French, 1906–1957) created drawings with the decalcomania technique. Surrealists embraced the idea of work that involved chance.

Organic Meets Geometric

Method: On graph paper, begin with an explosion—an ink spill, an ink blot—or blow ink across the paper's surface with a drinking straw. Extending out from the free-form explosion, develop it into geometric shapes and forms.

Goal: To combine organic and geometric shapes and forms into a coherent whole image

Model for Method: Gabriel Orozco (Mexican, b. 1962) is a sculptor, photographer and video artist. Some of his works start with a generative "explosion," an organic form. Using ink, for example, he then creates a geometric pattern around the organic forms. (http://www.tate.org.uk/context-comment/blog/gabriel-orozcos-extraordinary-drawings)

To see Orozco's work visit http://www.moma.org/interactives/exhibitions/2009/gabrielorozco.

Volume Through Line Direction

Method: Using groups of line moving in the same direction (hatching or something like hatching), describe planes of forms, or volumes, or rounded surfaces through direction and line weight.

Goal: Model form with visual texture and tone created by hatching lines

Model for Method: Vincent van Gogh (Dutch, 1853–1890)

Vincent van Gogh used hatching and crosshatching (groups of lines moving in the same direction that cross one another) to describe form and light. He also used different drawing tools including graphite, reed pen and quill in order to create a variety of marks such as dots, dashes and lines, which added great visual texture to his forms. Through placement and direction, van Gogh created the illusion of three-dimensional form and spaces as well as textures.

(To see van Gogh's drawings, visit: http://www.metmuseum.org/exhibitions/listings/2005/van-gogh-drawings). To learn more about his technique, visit: http://www.metmuseum.org/metmedia/interactives/art-trek/how-van-gogh-made-his-mark.

Type Glossary

TYPE CLASSIFICATION

A **serif** is a small semistructural stroke added to the upper or lower end of the main stroke of a character. The main classifications of serif typefaces are: Humanist, Transitional, Modern, Slab Serif and Blackletter. Within each classification, typefaces share some characteristics and structures.

Humanist or Old Style:

- Roman typefaces introduced in the late fifteenth century; most directly descended in form from letters drawn with a broad-edged pen
- **Characteristics:** stayed close to forms created by the chisel-edged pen; angled and bracketed serifs and biased stress
- **Examples:** Caslon, Garamond, Janson and Sabon

Transitional:

- Serif typefaces originating in the eighteenth century
- **Characteristics:** represent a transition from humanist to modern, exhibiting design characteristics of both
- **Examples:** Baskerville, Mrs Eaves and Georgia

Modern:

- Serif typefaces developed in the late eighteenth and early nineteenth centuries
- **Characteristics:** their form is more geometric in construction, as opposed to the humanist typefaces. Characterized by greatest thick–thin stroke contrast and vertical stress, they are the most symmetrical of all roman typefaces
- **Examples:** Didot, Bodoni and Walbaum

Slab Serif:

- Serif typefaces introduced in the early nineteenth century; subcategories are Egyptian and Clarendon
- **Characteristics:** heavy, slablike serifs
- **Examples:** American Typewriter, Memphis, ITC Lubalin Graph, Rockwell and Clarendon

Blackletter or Gothic:

- Typefaces based upon the thirteenth- to fifteenth-century medieval manuscript letterform. Gutenberg's first printing types were Textura, a blackletter style.
- **Characteristics:** a heavy stroke weight and condensed letters with few curves
- **Examples:** Textura, Rotunda, Schwabacher and Fraktur

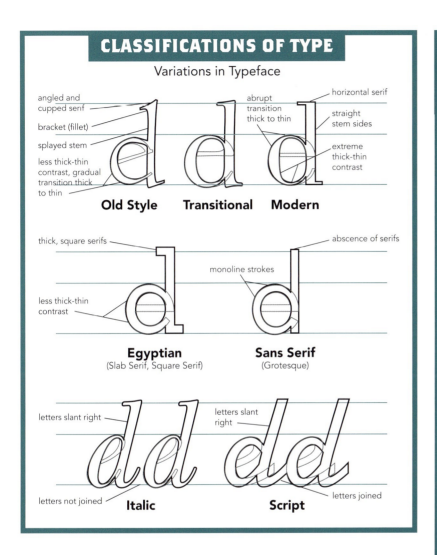

Type Checklist

Are the major characteristics that contribute to a typeface's voice appropriate for your visual identity? Evaluate a typeface based on shape, proportion, and balance.

- Proportions of the letterforms
- Shapes of the letterforms (rectilinear, curvilinear, geometric, or organic)
- Angle of stress
- Contrast between thick and thin strokes (or no contrast)
- Variation in line width
- Serif or sans serif
- Shape of serifs (bracketed or un-bracketed; triangular, flattened, tapering / almost vertical, pointed, hairline, thick, squared-off endings)

Sans serif typefaces are characterized by the absence of serifs and were introduced in the early nineteenth century; examples are Futura, Helvetica and Univers. Some letterforms without serifs have thick and thin strokes, such as Optima.

Humanist Sans Serif:

- **Characteristics:** sans serif typefaces with humanist characteristics and proportions; the most calligraphic of the sans serif typefaces
- **Examples:** Gill Sans. Some have thick/thin contrast, for example, Optima

Transitional Sans Serif:

The most common sans serif typefaces

- **Characteristics:** comparatively straight in appearance with less line width variation than Humanist sans serif typefaces. Some refer to this classification as "anonymous sans serif" because these type faces seem neutral or unadorned.
- **Examples:** Bell Centennial, Helvetica and Univers

Geometric Sans Serif:

- **Characteristics:** typefaces based on geometric shapes. The geometric shapes are apparent in the round letter *O* and single-story construction of the lowercase letter *a*. Often with little or no variation in stroke, geometric sans serif typefaces look modern or contemporary
- **Examples:** Futura and Century Gothic

Script:

These typefaces most resemble handwriting

- **Characteristics:** Letters usually slant and often are joined. Script types can emulate forms written with a flat-edged pen, flexible pointed pen (often called Copperplate), pencil or brush (associated with sign painting and show card lettering).
- **Examples:** Brush Script, Shelley Allegro Script and Snell Roundhand Script

Decorative:

Ornamental typefaces with very specific characteristics

- **Characteristics:** Some reference specific historical models, such as ornamental calligraphy, copperplate engravings, Chinoiserie and wood type. Decorative typefaces also include inlines, outlines and faceted and shadowed letters.
- **Caution:** They can overwhelm the visual communication with their own voices. Use decorative typefaces only in small doses for display and be very aware of what any decorative typeface references, whether era or fad.

Glossary of Terms

brand: the sum total of all characteristics and assets that differentiates it from the competition.

brand name: the main verbal differentiator for a product, service or group.

brand strategy: the core tactical underpinning of branding, uniting all planning for every visual and verbal application.

branding: the entire development process of creating a brand, brand name and visual identity, among other formats.

emotional benefit: an asset based on feelings and responses, not on a functional characteristic of a product or service.

functional benefit: the practical or useful characteristic of a product or service that aids in distinguishing a brand from its competition.

graphic interpretation: an elemental visualization of an object or subject, almost resembling a sign, pictogram or symbol in its reductive representation.

high contrast: a wide range of values.

hue: the name of a color; that is, red or green, blue or yellow.

icon: a generally accepted (pictorial or symbolic) visual used to represent objects, actions, and concepts. An icon resembles the thing it represents, or at minimum shares a quality with it. It can be a photograph, a pictorial representation, an elemental visual (think magnifying glass desktop icon), or arbitrary (think radioactive sign), or symbolic (think lightning bolt to represent electricity).

identity design: involves the creation of a systematic visual and verbal program intended to establish a consistent visual appearance and personality—a coordinated overarching identity—for a brand or group.

identity standards manual: guidelines for how the logo (and/or visual identity) is to be applied to numerous applications, from business cards to environmental design to vehicles to websites; also called a graphic standards manual.

integrated branding program: the creation of a comprehensive, strategic, unified and transmedia program for a brand.

letterform: the particular style and form of each individual letter of an alphabet.

lettering: the drawing of letterforms by hand (as opposed to type generated on a computer).

lettermark: a logo created using the initials of the brand or group name.

letterspacing: the spatial interval between letters.

light and shadow: employed to describe form; most closely simulates how we perceive forms in nature.

line: an elongated point, considered the path of a moving point; it also is a mark made by a visualizing tool as it is drawn across a surface.

line spacing or leading: spatial interval between two lines of type.

logo: a unique identifying symbol that represents and embodies everything a brand or company signifies. It provides immediate recognition; also called a brandmark, mark, identifier, logotype or trademark.

logotype: a logo that is an identifying mark where the name is spelled out in unique typography; also called word mark.

low contrast: a narrow range of values.

lowercase: the smaller set of letters. The name is derived from the days of metal typesetting when these letters were stored in the lower case.

Modern typeface: serif typeface, developed in the late eighteenth and early nineteenth centuries, whose form is more geometric in construction, as opposed to the Old Style typefaces, which stayed close to forms created by the chisel-edged pen.

modularity: a structural principle used to manage content using modules.

module: any single fixed element within a bigger system or structure; for example, a unit on graph paper, a pixel in a digital image, a rectangular unit in a grid system or a fixed encapsulated chunk of a composition.

naturalistic: a visual style created by full color or tone using light and shadow that attempts to replicate a subject as it is perceived in nature; also called realistic.

nonobjective: a purely invented visual, not derived from anything visually perceived; it does not relate to any object in nature and does not literally represent a person, place or thing; also called nonrepresentational.

notation: a linear, reductive visual that captures the essence of its subject, characterized by its minimalism.

Old Style: a roman typeface, introduced in the late fifteenth century, most directly descended in form from letters drawn with a broad-edged pen.

sans serif: typefaces characterized by the absence of serifs.

silhouette: the articulated shape of an object or subject taking its specificity into account (as opposed to the universal visual language of a pictograph).

strategy: the core tactical underpinning of any visual communication, unifying all planning for every visual and verbal application within a program of applications.

style: the quality that makes something distinctive.

symbol: a visual having an arbitrary or conventional relationship between the signifier and the thing signified.

symbol mark: a logo that is a pictorial, abstract or nonrepresentational visual or letterforms, which may or may not be coupled or combined with the brand name.

Transitional: a serif typeface, originating in the eighteenth century, that represents a transition from Old Style to Modern, exhibiting design characteristics of both.

type family: includes many style variations of a single typeface.

type style: variations of a typeface, which include variations in weight (light, medium, bold), width (condensed, regular, extended) and angle (roman or upright, and italic), as well as elaborations on the basic form (outline, shaded, decorated).

visual identity: the visual and verbal articulation of a brand or group, including all pertinent design applications, such as the logo, letterhead, business card and website, among others; also called brand identity and corporate identity.

Permissions

p. 10	Drew Davies quote used with permission. Drew Davies, Oxide Design Co. © 2013
p. 13	"Advice from Alberto Romanos" used with permission. Alberto Romanos © 2013
p. 15	Dany Lennon quote used with permission. Dany Lennon © 2013
p. 16	"Feature on Personal Branding" by Steve Liska used with permission. Steve Liska © 2013.
p. 17	Jaime Lynn Pecia quote used with permission. Jaime Lynn Pescia © 2013
p. 22	Linda Breskin quote used with permission. Linda Breskin © 2013.
p. 25	Alessandra Lariu quote used with permission. Alessandra Lariu © 2013.
p. 26	Interview with Dany Lennon used with permission. Dany Lennon © 2013.
p. 28	Prompt by Stephen T. Hall © 2013.
p. 30	Prompt by Richard Nochimson © 2013.
p. 32	Prompt by Drew Davies © 2013.
p. 35	Prompt by Suzanne Bousquet © 2013.
p. 41	Prompt by Megan Patrick © 2013.
p. 43	Prompt by Jull Bellinson © 2013.
p. 45	Suzanne Bousquet © 2013
p. 57	Kristen Campolattaro quote used with permission. Kristen Campolattaro © 2013
p. 68	Steve Liska quote used with permission. Steve Liska © 2013.
p. 73	Jaime Lynn Pecia quote used with permission. Jaime Lynn Pescia © 2013
p. 74	Interview with Laurence Vincent used with permission. Laurence Vincent © 2013.
p. 76	Interview with Rob Wallace used with permission. Rob Wallace © 2013.
p. 82	Prompt by Sean Adams © 2013.
p. 87	Prompt by Jaime Lynn Pescia © 2013.
p. 91, 94	Prompts by Paul Renner © 2013.
p. 105	Dean James Ballas quote used with permission. Dean James Ballas © 2013.
p. 110	Gui Borchert quote used with permission. Gui Borchert © 2013.
p. 110	Jaime Lynn Pescia quote used with permission. Jaime Lynn Pescia © 2013.
p. 127	Interview with Matteo Bologna used with permission. Matteo Bologna © 2013.
p. 130	Prompt by Melanie Wiesentha © 2013.
p. 132	Prompt by Jaime Lynn Pescia © 2013.
p. 137	Prompt by Nancy Novick © 2013.
p. 138	Prompt by Stephen T. Hall © 2013.
p. 139	Prompt by Julia Nevarez © 2013.
p. 143	Prompt by Stephen T. Hall © 2013.
p. 147	Prompt by Zandra Gratz © 2013.
p. 153	Prompt by Sean Adams © 2013.

Case Studies

Debbie Millman: all images used with permission. Debbie Millman © 2012.

Paul Renner: all images used with permission. Paul Renner © 2013.

Rich Arnold: all images used with permission. Rich Arnold © 2012.

Seunghyun Shon: all images used with permission. Seunghyun Shon © 2012.

Manik Rathee: all images used with permission. Manik Rathee © 2012.

Grace Duong: all images used with permission. Grace Duong © 2012.

Michael Sickenger: all images used with permission. Lava Dome Creative, LLC © 2012.

Kelly Thorn: all images used with permission. Kelly Thorn © 2013.

Kenny Barela: all images used with permission. Kenny J. Barela © 2010.

Jim Godfrey: all images used with permission. Jim Godfrey Design, LLC © 2012.

Jon Contino: all images used with permission. Jon Contino © 2012.

Allison Kerek: all images used with permission. Allison Kerek © 2012.

About the author

Robin Landa tells brand stories, designs, teaches, and presents at international conferences. She has won lots of awards (The National Society of Arts and Letters, The National League of Pen Women, Creativity, New Jersey Authors Award, the Art Directors Club of New Jersey, Graphic Design USA, Rowan University, Kean University, Carnegie Foundation "Great Teachers of Our Time", and she was a finalist in the Wall Street Journal's Creative Leaders competition) and has worn all-black since she was sixteen. She has written 18 books about branding, design, advertising, creativity, and drawing, including her first (but not last) children's book, The Dream Box, illustrated by Modern Dog Design Co.

Robin's numerous tomes include the bestseller Graphic Design Solutions, 5th edition, Essential Graphic Design Solutions, Advertising by Design, 2nd edition, Take A Line For A Walk: A Creativity Journal, and Designing Brand Experiences. You can read them in Chinese or Spanish, too.

With esteemed colleagues, Robin co-authored 2D: Visual Basics for Designers with Rose Gonnella and Steven Brower; Visual Workout with Rose Gonnella; and a set: Creative Jolt & Creative Jolt Inspirations with Denise Anderson and Rose Gonnella. (Stay tuned for Robin's next book, DRAW! A step-by-step guide to the basics of drawing.)

As a Distinguished Professor in the Robert Busch School of Design at Kean University, Robin has the opportunity to mentor very talented people who are forbidden to check their phones while she's lecturing unless they slip her some low-fat treats. Her students have gone on to successful visual communication careers; a few are featured in this book.

Robin has developed brand stories, designed, and written copy for Lava Dome Creative, among other design studios and ad agencies. Now, as creative director of her own firm, robinlanda.com, Robin works closely with marketing executives and their companies and organizations to develop brand strategy and stories as well as enhance corporate creativity through seminars. If you want to reach her to discuss design or life, you can find Robin on Twitter: @rlanda or at robinlanda.com or at rlanda@kean.edu.

Index

A
Absolut, 208
Adams, Sean, 82, 105, 153
AdamsMorioka, 82, 105, 153
Adobe Systems, 127
AIGA, 157
Aldine Press, 226
Alejo, Laura, 24
André Balazs Properties, 127
Anomaly, 162
Antonelli, Paola, 106
Apple, Inc., 174
Arnold, Rich, 166-169
    Facebook page, 167, 168
    logo, 169
    portfolio landing page, 169
    résumé, 167
    Twitter page, 167, 168
Arnold Worldwide, 162
AT&T, 174, 184
authenticity, brand strategy 13, 77
automatic drawing visualization technique, 58, 220
automatic writing visualization technique, 58, 59, 220
    See also free writing
automatism visualization technique, 220
Automatistes, les, 220
avatar, 110, 124

B
Ballas, Dean James, 105
Barela, Kenny, 190-193
    business card, 193
    infographic, 192
    label, 193
    promo materials, 191
    résumé, 193
Barnes & Noble, 127
Bearden, Romare, 221
Bellinson, Jill, 43
Blackletter/Gothic serif typefaces, 224
BMW, 162
Bologna, Matteo, 127
Borchert, Gui, 110, 208-213
    website, 210
    work samples, 209-211-213
Bousquet, Suzanne, 35, 45
brand, 228
    See also brand identity, personal; branding
brand building checklist, personal, 126
brand identity, personal, 15-21
    aesthetic vision and, 17
    altering, 16
    archetypes and, 18
    assets and, 16
    demonstration of, 21
    dual nature and, 19
    ethical virtues and, 20
    importance of, 26
    positive associations and, 19
    See also brand personality, evaluating; style
brand name, 228
brand personality, evaluating, 24
Brand Real, 74
brand strategy, 13, 228
    personal, 12-14
    See also authenticity, brand strategy and; consistency, brand strategy and; differentiation, brand strategy and; relevance, brand strategy
Brand Studio, United Talent Agency, The, 74
Brand Thinking and Other Noble Pursuits, 157, 161
brand voice, personal, 13, 60, 75
branding, 228

personal, 11-16
Breskin, Linda, 22, 68
Breton, André, 59
Breton's First Surrealist Manifesto, 59
Brower, Steven, 73
Budweiser, 162
business cards, 105, 121
   See also specific designers
Butler, Shine, Stern & Partners, 162

C

Cadbury, 208
Cambiaso, Luca, 219
Campbell, Joseph, 18
Campolattaro, Kristen, 57, 65
Carnival Cruise Lines, 162
CBS, 74
Chanel, Coco, 216
Cheston, Allison, 69, 118
Chwast, Seymour, 24
Clow, Lee, 73
clusters of marks visualization technique, 219
Coca Cola, 74, 184, 215
Colgate-Palmolive, 157, 184
collaboration, 24
collage painting visualization technique, 221
Collins, Brian, 104
color, 104, 114-117, 215
   See also color palette; color schemes; color wheel, pigment; colors; hue; saturation; temperature; value
color palette, 104, 117
   resume/letterhead/business card consistency, 118
   See also color schemes
color schemes, 116-117
   analogous, 116
   complementary, 116
   cool, 117
   monochromatic, 116
   split complementary, 116-117
   tetradic, 117
   triadic, 117
   warm, 117
   See also color palette
color wheel, pigment, 114
   See also color; color palette; color schemes; colors
colors
   achromatic, 114-115
   glossary of, 216-217
   interval, 114
   primary, 114
   prompts, 142
   secondary, 114
   See also color; color palettes; color schemes; color wheel, pigment
Colors: What They Mean and How to Make Them, 215
combination mark, 110
consistency, brand strategy and, 13, 56, 118
Contino, Jon, 198-202
   logos, 200
   promo piece, 199
   Twitter page, 201
   website, 202
continuously looping lines visualization technique, 221
Cotter, Holland, 222
cover letter, 72, 105
Creative Register, The, 15, 26
credibility, personal brand and, 75
Cudlin, Jeffrey, 219
curiosity, personal brand and, 76

D

Davies, Drew, 10, 32

decalcomania visualization technique, 223
Decorative sans serif typefaces, 227
Dell, 76
Design Management Institute, 76
"Design Matters with Debbie Millman," 157, 161
design sense, 107
design sensibility, 107
differentiation 13
Disney, 74
Disney Korea, 170
Doloff, Steven, 19
Domínguez, Oscar, 223
donnée prompt, 98
Duncan, Phil, 77
Duong, Grace, 180-183
    logo, 181
    résumé, 182
    work samples, 183
    Twitter page, 183

E

Eames, Charles, 104
Elements of Style, The, 60, 61, 62
elevator pitch, 57, 60, 64-65
    mapping and, 67
    opening line, 67
    prompt, 94
    using lists to craft, 68
    writing, 62-63, 77
emblem, 110
Emigre, 109
emotional benefit, 16, 228
ESPN, 162
"Essentials of Spontaneous Prose, The," 59
ethical virtues, personal brand identity and, 20
Experts.com, 77
Facebook, 73, 86, 154, 160, 167, 168, 175, 195
    See also specific designers
Fallon, 208
feedback, personal brand and, 75
Flavin, Dan, 219
Fletcher, Valerie J., 221
Four Seasons Hotels, 74
Fox Korea, 170
Fredrickson, Barbara, 106
free writing, 60
functional benefit, 16, 228

G

Ganesh, Chitra, 220
Garamound, Claude, 226
Geometric sans serif typefaces, 227
geometricize visualization technique, 219
Giacometti, Alberto, 221
Givaudan Fragrances, 184
Godfrey, Jim, 194-197
    Facebook page, 195
    logo, 195
    work samples, 195-197
Goodby, Silverstein & Partners, 162
Gottschall, Jonathan, 12, 74
graphic interpretation, 228
Gratz, Zandra, 147
Griffo, Francesco, 226
Gutenberg, 224

H

Hall, Stephen T., 28, 138, 143
Hallmark Cards, 204
Harley Davidson, 184
Hartung, Hans, 220
Hasbro, 157
Heinz, 76
Helberg, Simon, 73
Hemingway, Ernest, 62

Hero and The Outlaw, The, 18
Hero With a Thousand Faces 18
high contrast, 228
Hische, Jessica, 24
Hoefler & Frere-Jones, 109
Holtom, Gerald, 122
Home Depot, The, 74
HOW magazine, 41
How to Think Like a Great Graphic Designer, 157
hue, 114, 115-116, 228
Huge, Inc., 166
Humanist typefaces
    sans serif, 227
    serif, 224, 225, 226
    icon, 122, 123, 228
    prompts, 139, 151

I

identity. *See brand identity, personal*
identity design, 228
identity standards manual, 228
index, 122
Indiegogo.com, 24
Integer Group, The, 190
integrated branding program, 228
intellectual property, 124

J

Janson, Anton, 226
Jefferson, Thomas, 60
Jenkins, Henry, 105
Johnson & Johnson, 208
Jones, Pete, 73
Jordan, 162
Jung, Carl, 18

K

Kansas City Star stylebook, 62
KBS+P, 73
Kean University, 35, 139, 147, 170, 174
Kefico, 170
Kelly, Ellsworth, 222
Kerek, Allison, 204-207
    logo, 205
    résumé, 206
    website, 205, 207
Kerouac, Jack, 59
Kickstarter, 24
King, Stephen, 62, 63
Kipling, Rudyard, 64
Kusama, Yayoi, 222

L

Lariu, Alessandra, 25
Lauber, Margrethe, 73
leading, 228
Legendary Brands, 74
Lennon, Dany, 15, 26
letterform, 110, 228
letterhead, 119-121
    composition, 121
    design fundamentals, 120
    design process, 120
lettering, 228
lettermark, 110, 228
letterspacing, 228
light and shadow, 228
line, 228
line spacing, 228
    See also leading
LinkedIn, 65, 77
Liska, Steve, 16, 17, 68
Liska + Associates, 16, 17, 68
logo, 104, 108, 110-113, 228
    animated, 113
    elemental form, 112
    flat-shaped, 113
    free-form, 112
    high-contrast, 112
    linear, 112
    locked unit, 111
    prompts, 131-132, 136-137,

147-150, 152
resume/letterhead/business card consistency, 118
texture/pattern, 112, 113
three-dimensional-looking, 113
type and image relationships in, 111-113
unlocked unit, 111
volumetric, 112
See also specific designers; avatar; combination mark; emblem; lettermark; logotype; symbol
logotype, 110, 228
Look Both Ways, 157
Louise Fili Ltd, 184
low contrast, 229
lowercase, 229

M
Mad Man's Creed, 74
Mark, Margaret, 18
Marker Ski Bindings, 194
Masson, André, 220
MasterCard, 74
Mathieu, Georges, 220
Microsoft, 74
Millman, Debbie, 69, 118, 157-161

book cover, 161
Facebook page, 160
logos, 158
radio show promo piece, 161
Twitter page, 160
website, 159
mind map, 66-68
how to create, 67
prompt, 80
mind mapping, 66-68
automatic, 66, 67
deliberate, 66, 67
for elevator pitch, 67
mission statement, personal, 77
Modern serif typefaces, 224, 225, 226, 229
modularity, 229
module, 229
mood board prompt, 143
Morla, Jennifer, 24
Mother New York, 208
Mucca Design, 127

N
names and name system, 56-57
transmedia consistency, 56
naturalistic, 229
Nestlé, 76, 157

Nevárez, Julia, 139
New Balance, 208
NFL, 74
Nike, 208
Nochimson, Richard, 30
Nokia, 208
nonobjective, 229
notation, 229
Novick, Nancy, 137

O
Obama for America, 174
Old Style serif typefaces, 224, 225, 226, 229
Omnicom, 190
On Writing, 63
oral presentation tool technique, 21
organic meets geometric visualization technique, 223
Orozco, Gabriel, 223
Osborn, Alex,
Oxide Design Co., 10, 32

P
Parker, Dorothy, 60
passion, personal brand and, 75
Path to Purchase Institute, 76
Patina Restaurant Group, 127

Patrick, Megan Lane, 41
patterns of dots visualization technique, 222
Pearson, Carol S., 18
Pepsi, 157, 184
Personal Life Map, 35
personal projects, 24
personality. *See brand personality, evaluating*
Pescia, Jaime Lynn, 17, 79, 87, 110, 132
Pfizer, 76
Picasso, Pablo, 217
pitch. *See elevator pitch*
Pizza Hut, 162
Pratt, 19
Print magazine, 157
Proctor and Gamble, 76, 77, 157, 184
PUMA Football, 208

R

R/GA, 208
Rathee, Manik, 174-179
    blog, 177
    Facebook profile, 175
    logo, 175
    résumé, 175
    Twitter profile, 175, 178
    website, 178
    work samples, 176
Reckitt Benckiser, 184
reductive line visualization technique, 222
reflection, personal brand and, 75
relevance, brand strategy and, 13, 75, 77
Renner, Paul, 91, 94, 162-165
    logo, 163
    website, 163-165
résumé, 69-72, 104, 105, 118-119, 127
    contents of conventional, 70-72
    design approaches, 118-119
    goals, 69, 118
    sample, 70-71
    tips, 72, 119
    See also specific designers
RevSystems, Inc., 174
Rizzoli, 127
Romanos, Alberto, 13
Rosenberg, Karen, 222

S

Samsung, 170
sans serif typefaces, 227, 229
    See also Decorative sans serif typefaces; Geometric sans serif typefaces; Humanist typefaces; Script sans serif typefaces; Transitional typefaces
saturation (color), 114, 115, 116
Savannah College of Art and Design, 28, 138, 143
Schapiro, Meyer, 23
Scher, Paula, 24
Schneider, Gérard, 220
School of Visual Arts, 157
Script sans serif typefaces, 225, 227
Sega, 162
serif typefaces, 224-226
    characteristics, 226
    classifications, 224
    See also Blackletter/Gothic serif typefaces; Humanist typefaces; Modern serif typefaces; Old Style serif typefaces; Slab Serif typefaces; Transitional typefaces
Seunghyun Shon, 124, 170-173

business cards, 173
logo, 171
résumé, 171
website, 172
72andSunny, 110, 208
Shakespeare, William, 30
SheSays, 25
Sickinger, Michael, 184-185
    résumé, 185
    website, 185
sign, 122
signs/symbols/icons, system of, 118, 122
    See also icon; index; sign; symbol
silhouette, 229
skills prompt, 31
Slab Serif typefaces, 224, 225, 226
Snapple, 184
social media
    personal branding and, 77
    prompt, 86
    See also Facebook; LinkedIn; Twitter
sociogram prompt, 45
Something of Myself, 64
Sontag, Susan, 23
Sony PlayStation, 74

Soulages, Pierre, 220
spontaneous art, 58, 220
spontaneous writing, 58, 59, 220
    See also free writing
Sposato, John, 109
Sprint, 174
Starr Restaurants, 127
Sterling Brands, 69, 118, 157
story, personal brand
    determining premise of, 61-62
    visualizing, 104-109
    See also storytelling
storytelling, 60-63
    personal branding and transmedia, 12, 74, 104-105
    See also story, personal brand
Storytelling Animal, The, 12
strategy, 229
    See also brand strategy, personal
Strunk, Jr., William, 61, 62
style, 23, 229
    finding authentic personal, 22-23
"Style," 23
Suburu, 162
SUM, 190
Sun Valley, 194

symbol, 110, 122, 124, 229
    abstract, 110
    character icon, 110
    glossary, 218-219
    letter form, 110
    nonrepresentational, 110
    pictorial, 110
    prompts, 132, 148-150
    See also avatar
symbol mark, 229
Syrup New York, 208

T

Tachists, 220
Target, 127
temperature (color), 115-116
terms, glossary of, 228-229
Thorn, Kelly, 186-189
    business card, 188
    invoice, 189
    logo, 187
    résumé, 187
    thank you card, 189
    website, 188
Transitional typefaces
    sans serif, 225, 227
    serif, 224, 225, 226, 229
transmedia storytelling, personal

branding and, 12, 74, 104-105
Twitter, 86, 155, 160, 167, 168, 175, 178, 183, 201
    personal brand and, 73
    profile/bio, 60, 73
    See also specific designers
Tyler School of Art, Temple University, 186, 204
Type Directors Club, 127
type family, 229
type style, 229
typeface
    design, 106
    prompts, 128-130, 133-135
    See also sans serif typefaces; serif typefaces; typefaces
typefaces
    aesthetic considerations in selecting, 108
    functional considerations in selecting, 108
    pairing, 109, 127
    resume/letterhead/business card consistency, 118
    selecting, 107-108
    See also sans serif typefaces; serif typefaces; typeface; typography
typography, 107
    color temperature and, 116

U

unique selling proposition (USP), 57, 65
USP. *See unique selling proposition (USP)*

V

value (color), 114, 115, 116
Van Gogh, Vincent, 223
Varichon, Anne, 215
verbal brand, crafting, 66-68
    See also mind map; mapping, mind
Victoria's Secret, 127
Vignelli, Massimo, 107
Vincent, Laurence, 74-75
visual identity, 229
visualization techniques, 219-223
    See also specific visualization techniques
vitaminwater, 74
voice. *See brand voice, personal*
Volkswagen, 162
volume through line direction visualization technique, 223

W

W+K, 162
Wallace, Rob, 76-77, 118
Wallace Church, Inc., 76, 118
website, personal, 57, 104, 105, 125
    brand positioning and, 57
    grid structure, 125
    homepage, 125
    tips, 124
    See also specific designers
Wiesenthal, Melanie, 130, 146
Will a Graphic Résumé Get You the Job? The Experts Respond, 69, 118
Wols, Frans, 220
writing. *See automatic writing visualization technique; free writing; spontaneous writing*
Wu-ki, Zao, 220

Y

Yellowstone National Park, 194

More Great Titles from HOW Books

ARCHETYPES IN BRANDING
BY MARGARET POTT HARTWELL & JOSHUA C. CHEN

Archetypes in Branding: A Toolkit for Creatives and Strategists gives you an effective and incredibly practical tool for branding and marketing. Using a highly participatory approach to branding strategies, combined with sixty beautiful (and incredibly useful) brand archetype cards, this kit offers you a creative and intuitive tool for charting a course for your brand.

BLOGGING FOR CREATIVES
BY ROBIN HOUGHTON

It's imperative for all good designers to have an online presence that starts with a great blog. While blogging software has become user-friendly and packed with features, it still pays to put thought into your blog's design, features, posting capabilities and written content. *Blogging for Creatives* teaches you how to start a blog that readers will return to. You'll learn how to design, publish, host and maintain your blog. Once you're up and running, you'll learn about making it work for you, keeping it fresh, staying motivated and forging connections in the blogosphere.

SPECIAL OFFER FROM HOW BOOKS!

You can get 15% off your entire order at MyDesignShop.com! All you have to do is go to www.howdesign.com/howbooks-offer and sign up for our free e-newsletter on graphic design. You'll also get a free digital download of HOW magazine.

 For more news, tips and articles, follow us at Twitter.com/HOWbrand

 For behind-the-scenes information and special offers, become a fan at Facebook.com/HOW-magazine

 For visual inspiration, follow us at Pinterest.com/HOWbrand

FIND THESE BOOKS AND MANY OTHERS AT MYDESIGNSHOP.COM OR YOUR LOCAL BOOKSTORE.